About the Author

Gill Hester has lived in various places in Buckinghamshire all her life. A working mother fighting the battle of the bulge. Running her own business, she has led an interesting and varied life having travelled the world. Loves horses, skiing, hiking and food!

Gastric Band
My
Silent Friend

GILL HESTER

authorHOUSE®

AuthorHouse™ UK Ltd.
500 Avebury Boulevard
Central Milton Keynes, MK9 2BE
www.authorhouse.co.uk
Phone: 08001974150

First published by AuthorHouse 5/30/2008

ISBN: 978-1-4343-6917-8 (sc)

Printed in the United States of America
Bloomington, Indiana

This book is printed on acid-free paper.

Contents

Chapter 1

Depressed, Obese & Couch Potato

My final attempt to become slim aged 51 – 52 next month the last hope my dieting diary.

9th November 2004 at 10.45am - I have decided to give Dr Watt my GP a call, to see if I can make an appointment for a consultation with someone regarding having a gastric band fitted, to stop me over-eating. This might sound appalling but I have tried absolutely every diet you can think of from Weight-Watchers, Rosemary Connelly, to having my teeth wired in my early 20's so I could be light enough to race/ride, exercising regularly at the gym, running round the fields, doing exercises on my own, using the running machine at home, you name it I have tried it and I just cannot keep the weight off. The adjustable laparoscopic gastric band is supposed to last for 10 years, well if it does I will be 62 by the time it has stopped working, so with a bit of luck I would have 10 years without having the worry of being fat. I am probably as fat as I have ever been.

Appointment made with Dr Watt for Monday 15th November 2004 at 8.30am.

Having seen Dr Watt, who looked at me as if he understood (and not as if I was mad), he told me only last week he had been to a lecture given by Mr Appleton, a general surgeon consultant who carries out the gastric band placement surgery in Buckinghamshire. So he is going to make me an appointment to see Mr Appleton at The Paddocks Hospital. I look forward to hearing from him.

22nd November, haven't heard anything from Mr Appleton so rung The Paddocks Hospital today and his secretary is coming back to me. It is now 6pm on the 22nd November, Mr Appleton's secretary Jackie has just called to say that Mr Appleton will see me tomorrow evening at 6pm at The Paddocks. I feel quite excited because it feels like the end of an era for me.

Tuesday 23rd November and my appointment is at 6pm. I left home just after 5pm and arrived at The Paddocks a couple of minutes early. I saw Mr Hanley, who looked after Bill [my late husband] when he had the tumour on his spine and had a good chat with him. Mr Appleton came out to greet me and I have to say he looks a nice, kind guy.

An hour and a half later, it is now 7.30pm and I have just come out from seeing Mr Appleton. After an examination he had a long talk with me and told me all about the gastric band. He said there is a 15% chance of it slipping once fitted. He also weighed and measured me, stating that I am only just big enough to have this operation. He would prefer me to be a little bigger to justify operating on me however, he decided he would go ahead because my mother was a diabetic who also had heart problems and died at the age of 57. So, I think I am going to go ahead. I feel quite nervous but I have information to read about the procedure and I am going to look into it in some depth. He did ask if I was 100% happy with him and whether I would speak to other patients looking to have this procedure, I said I would.

He has given me notes explaining I would be on a puree diet for approximately six weeks, that I will be unable to drive for a week, and also two weeks before the operation I must not eat anything containing fat. I am definitely thinking of having it done, my next step is to see the dietician.

14th December, I sent Mr Appleton a letter because I had not heard from the dietician. I also asked a couple of questions, one being if Mr Farouk would operate with him, as I have decided two heads are better than one, also to inform him I am allergic to penicillin and terrified of the anaesthetic. But he will, I am sure, speak with the anaesthetist beforehand to let him know I am petrified of being put to sleep.

20th December, at long last I have heard from the dietician and my appointment is at 7pm tonight at the Chiltern Hospital.

I have met with Jane the dietician who is very pleasant. She has gone through everything I eat, what I don't eat, and weighed me again. She explained more about the gastric band, the people she has seen, and how it is very important to have your husband's support 100%. Well I have that as Steve is very supportive about me having it done. I spent approximately an hour and a half with Jane and I have to say she is very thorough. She told me she would come and see me in hospital once the operation had been carried out and visit my home on a regular basis, to make sure I have the necessary nutritional intake, because constipation can be a major problem if enough water isn't taken. You can also become very tired if you do not have multi-vitamins.

I left The Chiltern feeling as if I am definitely going to go ahead. I think I will speak to Mr Appleton's secretary tomorrow to book the operation.

23rd December and I still haven't booked the operation. I feel very nervous about it, it is a very drastic thing to do, inside I definitely want to go ahead but nerves are telling me not to do it. £7,200 is a lot of money, can I really justify spending that amount to stop me eating? [especially when thousands are starving....I feel guilty about the money] but if I look at it over a period of 10 years it is only about £600 a year to stop me eating, and I will save £7,000 easily in food alone if it works and have peace of mind! Having sat at the top of a mountain all day in Obergurgl, Austria with no energy to ski eating and drinking all day long – at this rate I will die of a heart attack. Have made a positive decision to book the operation on my return to the UK.

4th January 2005 I am going to ring up and book my appointment today to go into the Shelburne Wycombe private hospital, where Mr Appleton carries out the gastric banding procedure. I have made a positive decision to go ahead. I had decided on Wednesday the 19th January but Mr Appleton is already fully booked for that day, so I have now booked for January 26th which will allow me a full week off work before I have to resume telemarketing.

I have told very few people about the pending operation. I have told Wendy who is very supportive, Debbie because I need her to look after the office while I am poorly, and Sandra who I think was pretty shocked. Lisa was mortified, so I will not be mentioning it to her again until after I have had it done. I spoke to Thomas and he is very supportive as well. It is very important to me that Steve and Thomas support my decision. Not too concerned about anyone else, but don't want to worry people so I shall now keep it to myself. I am really looking forward to having this procedure carried out in order to keep my weight under control again, and not be constantly feeling like an unattractive beached whale.

12th January and only two weeks to go until the procedure is carried out, I feel very excited about it. Glad I have made the decision - won't be long now! I must be getting pretty nervous because I have been binging heavily, a true trait of me worrying about something. I have been to Tesco's for the last three days and stuffed myself with jacket potatoes, baked beans, cheese & butter. I must stop doing this because Mr Appleton asked me not to eat any fat for the fortnight before I have the operation so that is my last treat today. I must restrict myself otherwise I will make his job incredibly difficult. I note in his letter he states my weight is 13 stone 1lb or 83.2kg and my height is only 4'11 or 150cms which gives me a body mass of 37, this is classified as obese, and if my weight increases further to a body mass of greater than 40, I would be at serious risk. So I am almost morbidly obese and the likes of diabetes, high blood pressure, and worsening of arthritis would be serious things for me to worry about. However, at the moment I do not have any of these apart from arthritis, so I am hoping the surgery will really help me. I am very, very excited about it even though I am terrified. I am hoping to have lost 3 stones by the summer, which I know will be a bit quick, but I am hoping to wear little tops again with my skinny jeans I have been unable to get into since I came back from Greece about 3 years ago. I am hoping this really works, please God let it work, and help me to remain as slim as I would like to for the rest of my days.

One thing I must not do is drink water with my food any longer. I must drink it before or after I have my dinner but not while I am eating food. I can't remember if I mentioned I have started on the chewable vitamins, they taste disgusting, but they are something I am going to have to take for the rest of my life so I need to get used to them.

Having measured 5 to 6 tablespoons of yogurt into a little bowl to see what my evening meal will be like in the future, it doesn't look a lot, so if I don't lose three stones in six months I shall be very disappointed. Time will tell.

15th January and it is four o'clock in the morning, unable to sleep, having disturbed dreams, the multi-vitamin tablets seem to be giving me a bit of irritation under my skin. I feel restless, bit nervous and will be very glad when the next week and a half has passed and I have had the operation. I am having disturbing dreams and unable to return back to sleep which is very irritating. I keep reading the information about the operation and would just like it to be over.

19th January, woke up at half past five with the operation very much on my mind. I am very worried about the constipation situation. The chewable vitamins are well into my system so I don't have any unknown side effects once I have had the operation. I am a little spotty on the face and slightly constipated so whether they will suit me or whether they have too much iron in them I am not too sure. When I saw the nutritionist she did say this can be a problem. Constipation can be very painful so I am hoping when I speak to the nutritionist again she will be able to help. I learned yesterday that I have to go to the hospital for an hour tomorrow, [Thursday] to have blood tests and I imagine I will also see the anaesthetist to prepare me for what is going to happen next Wednesday.

A week to go now and feeling very nervous. I paid for the operation yesterday because I had a letter arrive informing that you are supposed to pay 10 days beforehand if you are not insured, and of course no insurance will cover this type of operation at the moment. I think it is short sighted because people who are overweight develop nasty things like diabetes and are more prone to arthritis, well arthritis being aggravated.

Also booked a holiday yesterday to Egypt to stay at The Four Seasons Hotel, really looking forward to this because it will be hot and give me a chance to have a bit of a tan for the summer months. I am hoping by the time I go on the 25th April I will have lost a minimum of two stones as it is three months away. I keep thinking ...... will I fit back into a bikini? Highly unlikely, but at least I will be able to walk without my legs rubbing together and my knees knocking. Also, without the rolls of fat hanging down my back and off my bust, so all positive thinking even though I am terrified. Hopefully the double chins will have disappeared as well by then. Steve has come out of the bedroom this morning and caught me with a sausage sandwich made with three sausages and thick butter. I am not supposed to be having any fat, I don't think he was too amused but my justification of pigging like this is that I am not going to be able to do it for much longer. For my own sake I shouldn't be doing it, but thoroughly enjoyed the sandwich all the same, even though feeling very guilty.

I have now filled out the pre-op assessment and admission forms to take with me tomorrow.

20th January and been down to The Shelburne Hospital, High Wycombe for my pre-operation blood test, weigh in, heart check, and blood pressure check. I asked the nurse, who was very nice, questions about other people who have had the operation. She gathered I was very nervous about the anaesthetic and told me I was very small to be having the operation compared to other women she had seen. But I explained to her that I didn't want to be battling the bulge for the rest of my days, I feel so strongly about it that I want to do something very positive and not have the worry of it any longer. I had a very good hour and a half down there and feel much better for having that part of it out of the way. The last time I went to High Wycombe hospital was to have Thomas so hopefully the visit this time will be as successful as back in 1980!!

I have been to Ford, the physio today in Gloucester, told him about the op and he was quite stunned I had decided to take such drastic action, but he fully understood why and said he was very proud of me for making such a positive decision to do something about an ever increasing problem. He said long term I should really benefit from it and probably feel years younger, and I am sure I will. So, all good positive stuff. I had acupuncture, which I don't normally like, but today I felt it did some good, it made me relax. He also worked my shoulder, hip and neck which have been aching, so it has been a long day but a productive one. Roll on next Wednesday the 26th.

Steve has taken eight pictures of me stood in my bra and pants at different angles in the doorway arch … a bit of memorabilia from before the operation. I look forward to having six taken in three months time to see if I have shrunk much, hopefully I will have.

21st January woke up early in the morning and feel disorientated this morning, slight stomach ache, and moody. I have had mood swings all day. I haven't got on very well productively, been messing around, totally unorganized and just haven't been able to get my act together. Went out for a meal at The Mole and Chicken, our last Friday night out together which we normally enjoy and it was disastrous. The food was good, but with my mood swings Steve had a job to cope with me and we didn't have a very good time so that was sad. Anyway, let's hope tomorrow brings better things.

22nd January and have been to London to see Thomas who was looking well, and to visit the French exhibition at Olympia. Thoroughly enjoyed it, had lunch at TGI Friday's and it suddenly hit me how much fried food is served in there. I normally love TGI Friday's but today I have to say I didn't particularly enjoy it. I did have a cheese beef burger and what with the fat I ate yesterday, two bars of chocolate and roast duck, I have had two very fatty days. I am supposed to be on low fat so not very good! It was wonderful to see Thomas, the exhibition was good and I brought loads of literature home. It will give me something to think about. I haven't felt so moody today and on the whole enjoyed myself and looking forward to the operation. Thomas said that all anaesthetics have to be taken seriously of course, I don't think he is worried at all about me having it done he understands why I am going ahead and roll on Wednesday. I definitely feel more positive today about everything.

I have bought some more nightwear today to wear in hospital, one set of grey pyjamas, one black nightdress and one set of shorts & t-shirt, but I think I look best in the grey pyjamas but we will watch this space and wait and see, anyway I have enough gear to go into hospital.

23rd January and my last Sunday before I have the operation, it is a beautiful, bright, sunny day and I feel more or less on top of the world, really looking forward to the operation, hence having had bad mood swings earlier in the week. I have organized myself, have written a list of what I am going to take into hospital with me, have been back to Tesco and bought myself another pair of jersey cotton pyjamas to wear and also some slippers because these are not things I wear on a regular basis. So I am organized. I ate half a paella, not because I was hungry but because I love the stuff and I just feel I am not going to be able to eat much of it after my operation, so it is like a last minute indulgence - yet another one. By the time I go in I shall be twice the size I am now at the rate I'm going with all these last minute treats! I also had a bar of chocolate which I definitely shouldn't have had, but remembering what the nurse said – no sucking and no sipping, in other words no sucking chocolate and no sipping alcohol. The alcohol doesn't bother me but the chocolate definitely does. I bought a funny little pair of slippers, they are purple because that was the only colour they had, never likely to use them again after I have been in so wasn't much point in spending a fortune on them.

It is starting to hit me how little I am going to be able to eat, five tablespoons is barely one Mueller light yogurt pot size, so I am certainly going to be cheap to keep from Wednesday onwards.

Monday 24th January and I have got up bright and breezy, taken the dogs for a walk, the last time I will do that before I go in for my operation because I feel as if I could possibly have a cold coming and I don't want to tempt fate by going out in the freezing cold air. It was minus three this morning and I definitely felt very cold. It has also been cold in the office, I had to come in and put another jumper on so don't want to be ill for Wednesday or they won't operate on me. Last time of walking the dogs and only one more day to go in the office but I have done the bulk of the work today. I had a bar of chocolate today which I shouldn't have had and also a very small bread and butter pudding. The low fat has really gone badly and I hope I am not going to suffer because I haven't been able to cut it right back.   However I will be honest with Mr Appleton and tell him that I have continued to eat fatty food. I have been watching a programme on silicone and how it can affect the body, and of course the band is actually made of silicone so time will tell whether it is successful or not or whether it will poison my system like silicone based breast implants can. I must remember to ask Mr Appleton what happens to the band after ten years, I probably should have asked this earlier on. They say it lasts for ten years but I don't know whether I have to have it removed or whether it dissolves, which is doubtful, although I think silicone breasts disintegrate after ten years, so I must ask what happens.

25th January and woke at ten to six. I have weighed in at 13 stone just before my operation. My measurements are as follows – bust 43", waist 38", widest part 45", hips 43", left thigh 24", right thigh 24", left knee 17", right knee 17", left arm 14", right arm 13½". These measurements are much bigger than when I went on my world trip. When I returned from my world trip my measurements were – bust 40", waist 33½", widest part 40", hips 38½", left thigh 21", right thigh 20½", left knee 12½", right knee 13", left arm 12½", right arm 12" so a substantial increase since I returned 18 months ago.

Today I have a busy day getting all the work up together and being fully prepared to go in and leave home at half past six tomorrow morning. The photographs Steve took of me in the doorway are still being developed and won't be ready until tomorrow. This is too late so we have to do them again this morning as I have to take them with me.

9.30pm in the evening on the 25th January and it is my final night before I have my operation. Because we were away at Christmas Steve and I had our Christmas dinner tonight - we had turkey, pigs in blankets, cranberry sauce, sage & onion, cauliflower, cabbage and peas, mash, new potatoes and a couple of glasses of beautiful red wine. The day has been pretty troublesome but the evening has been extremely pleasant. Had the notice of one tenant today, giving up 4,500 square feet so that is a bit of a downer on going into hospital tomorrow, but we live to fight another day and what does it really matter it is only money – she says, tongue in cheek!

Jane, the nutritionist rang me tonight to wish me luck and to say that she would see me on Thursday so that was nice. I had a chat with her and also with Wendy and I am looking forward to it all being over now.

Chapter 2

Gastric Band Operation & Recovery

26th January and it is three o'clock in the morning, aged 52, the day has arrived. I have three and a half hours before I leave home, woke up feeling very nervous, slightly nauseous and basically scared. I have the television on, I can't read my book, I have made a note to tell the anaesthetist about my loose tooth and I shall just be so glad when it is all over. I am petrified this morning, wondering if I have made the right decision but in 2 months time I am sure I will have made the right decision. I desperately want to loose the fat, especially having seen the before photographs Steve has taken of me where I look like an all-in wrestler. It will all be over soon - we leave home at 6.30am.

I have my band on my arm saying what I am having done and who I am having it done by. I have been told Mr Appleton and the anaesthetist will be in any time between now and 8.30am.

8.30am I am putting on my gown and paper knickers ready for the off. Mr Appleton has been in to see me at nine o'clock. Signed the consent form and I have to say he is very nice, he is good looking, very smart and good bedside manner so I am quite relaxed regarding the operation, but I am very nervous of the anaesthetic. It is quarter past nine now and the anaesthetist has been to see me, a nice

Indian gentleman who works at Stoke Mandeville. He is not going to give me a pre-med so I feel really nervous. He has told me that if the loose tooth I have on the bottom gum gets knocked he might have to pull it out, so I hope he doesn't knock it and it remains where it is because it's hardly loose at all and I don't really fancy having a gap. I am now about to put on these lovely stockings with this gown and paper pants, sounds gorgeous doesn't it. I am now stood here looking like an absolute lemon - I have certainly looked better! No turning back now the porter has come to collect me for theatre. It seems a long walk but it will soon be over.

8.15 at night and I have been visited by Mr Appleton who said the operation went well, very neat, they had to put the balloon port at my side instead of above my chest bone so he was very pleased. I will see him tomorrow and after I am discharged I shall see him a week after that. I told him I have been keeping a diary, photographs have been taken and developed and he would like a copy for his future patients. Steve and Thomas were here so I had two lovely visitors tonight and lots of kisses from both of them. Obviously they were both relieved to see that I am ok and I had a lovely time with them both. I am now out of bed and feel pretty chipper, the only problem is I can't have a wee which I would like to do. I have drunk three quarters of a litre of water so I am getting a little bit worried. The house doctor is going to see me so we will wait and see what she has to say. On the whole life is pretty good. I have these air things on my legs which pulsate as if I am running, so I suppose I have had a little bit of a run today even though I haven't!

The time now is quarter past nine in the evening and I am having pain killers soon as I am starting to get a bit of discomfort. I am going to see if I can have another go at having a wee. I shall run the tap to see if that helps at all like I used to do with the horses. It is now half past ten and I have just had Paracetamol and Voltarol in my bottom, so definitely getting the works. My hand is bandaged with a lead in it with a drip because I kept catching it. I look as if I have really been in the wars. At least the catheter is not too uncomfortable. My legs have bicycle pump things on again and I feel as if I am running the marathon at the same time.

27th January 5.30 in the morning, I have been woken up from a deep sleep after having had a sleeping pill but being checked throughout the night. I had my blood pressure taken, given antibiotics and pain killers and had the plasma bag changed again. I do feel a bit sore this morning. I have also pressed the bed to sit me up to have a glass of water. I am hoping when Mr Appleton comes around at eight o'clock I can have the catheter out and try to go to the loo naturally. Seven o'clock and I have had a wash, cleaned my teeth and a spot of perfume, definitely feeling much brighter than earlier on. The pain is nothing like it was, although it was more of a dull ache than an actual pain so I feel I am well on the mend. Just hope the waterworks sort themselves out.

It is now nine o'clock I have had the catheter removed and taken my water tablet. I am now back on the drip unfortunately but it looks as if I am staying on that for the day, definitely won't be going home today, so the nurse says, but I have the dietician coming in at ten o'clock and we will wait until Mr Appleton comes in at lunchtime.

It is 12 noon and I have had a very busy morning, I spoke to Thomas briefly and told him I am ok. I spoke to Steve and Guinness (one of our dogs) managed to run off while I was talking to him. The dietician visited and went through all I have to do for the next few days. I can now have a cup of hot chocolate or something like that in order to start me off on other things besides clear water and by the end of the week I can be on thick soups. I can have very thin soup today so we will just see how we go. I have spoken to Wendy who told me she has not been too well which is a bit worrying but hopefully she will be better soon. The physio visited twice but she had to go away again each time because the dietician was still here. The nurse has been back in and taken down the drip so we are making progress, although I still have the needle in my hand.

I have had my first half cup of Horlicks and I have to say it tasted very sweet and sickly, but I am very glad of it because I have been dying for something warm and my stomach has been really churning. After having been eating like a pig for the last god knows how long to suddenly going without having anything to eat or drink apart from water, my stomach has obviously thought that my throat has been cut, but in fact it is my stomach that has been cut in half not my throat. The vegetable soup was absolutely lovely. It is now ten to four on my first day of having the banding and I had some soup for lunch. I am having another cup of hot Ovaltine for tea time. I had some beautiful flowers delivered from Lisa and went for another walk down the passageway and back. Feeling good, and passing wind which has made me feel better!!

Mr Appleton has been in and said I can go home. Steve has arrived to take me home. I have had more soup, some Ovaltine and a little yogurt as well. Had a bit of a shock when I put my jeans on, they won't do up so I had to go home in my jogging bottoms. It was very cold walking from the hospital to the car, didn't realise just how weak I am. Looking at myself in the car mirror I look absolutely dreadful, even though I felt really good while I was in the hospital. We have driven home and going over the bumps in the new road which is being laid outside Bicester was pretty painful but now I am home and indoors and sitting on my own bed I feel much better.

28th January, my first morning home and I am awake at four o'clock and feel a little tender around my tummy, it also feels a touch tight. I managed to go to the loo alright so that is one consolation and took some Paracetamol. Definitely didn't realise just how much the Voltarol was keeping the pain away. I wouldn't really say I hurt, I am just a little bit frightened to move, I feel as if I am made of porcelain, frightened I will stretch it or something. Also sleeping in my own bed I have slept more upright than I did in the hospital so I probably haven't been as comfortable as I would have liked. I had to take a sleeping tablet last night just to help me relax and settle into being back at home. I do look a bit like death warmed up this morning, big black circles under the eyes, but I am so relieved I have had it done. I have woken up this morning not feeling hungry so that is even better. Normally I would have got up and had a cheese sandwich or something from the fridge, or cereal of some kind, so that is definitely a vast improvement.

I had a bit of phlegm on my chest and I am sure sleeping upright has helped move that because I haven't had to cough really hard to move it so that is one good thing. It does seem terrible I have just spent £7,200 on stopping eating when the Auschwitz concentration camp is constantly being shown on the television for its 60th Anniversary where people were starving. It just shows how times have changed.

It is now eight o'clock and I have taken a couple more Paracetamol, read a bit of my Victoria Beckham book and I have to say I feel really rough. I had a cup of hot milk and that made me feel a little bit better but right now I am beginning to wonder what I have done. My stomach is just so swollen. Mr Appleton said I would have a few down days and I think today is going to be one of those. Probably should have stayed in hospital for another day I think. 9.30pm and getting near my bedtime. It has been a long day and had mood swings on and off all day. Jane the dietician came to see me and she said my liquids are good. Mr Appleton has phoned to make sure I am alright which was nice. I have definitely had a funny sort of day, feel very sorry for myself off and on and I am hoping tomorrow will be better. Had some yogurt, hot chocolate, tomato soup and a litre and a half of water today. The Paracetamol tablets I am having to take every four hours are making me feel sick and the Nurofen Steve has got for me isn't doing much else other than making me feel sick either. Ten o'clock and bed time, I am crawling into bed with my sexy white stockings on, these fancy stockings have to remain on for another week, true passion killers!

28th January at 6.00am and a much better night last night, have woken up this morning in the early hours coughing with a little bit of phlegm on my chest and very pleased to say that my bowels have now opened so I feel much more comfortable, the simple things in life are the best! I have taken my Paracetamol and Codeine.

My neck and shoulders do not feel any where near as stiff as they did yesterday and I think the heated wheat bag has definitely helped, Steve massaging the base of my neck last night has also probably helped.

It is now 8.30 in the evening I have had a pretty good day. I am glad I had some exercise walking around the paddock, and this evening, because I was feeling a little sick when Steve got back from London, I had a walk around the site again and the fresh air seemed to do me a power of good. My hands are still very swollen and I had a little bit of discomfort but I am drinking well. I have had terrible cravings for things that I really like, like shepherd's pie and sausages and crusty bread rolls, but obviously haven't had any of them at all because it would be absolutely stupid to do so. It just shows how my mind is constantly working on food, food and more food. It is such a relief to think that I won't be able to stuff myself with food any more once the band has settled and I have healed properly. Early to bed at 8.30pm tonight because I do feel tired.

30th January at 6.00a.m and woke up with a little bit of pain so have taken the horrible Paracetamol and Nurofen. I have been to the loo and still have terrible wind, not very pleasant, hope that is going to subside. My stomach is rumbling for all its worth and I hope that is going to stop as well. My shoulders are aching a little from sitting up, however I am really looking forward to losing the weight. All these negative things are a small price to pay if I am going to be slim.

It is 9.00am and after having taken a shower I stood in front of the mirror to look at the small incisions Mr Appleton has carried out on my stomach. I would say today I am not so swollen, now whether that is because my stomach is going down because I am on very limited amounts of food intake, or whether it is the swelling going down I am not too sure but the bruising is coming out. I look a little as if I have been in the ring with Mike Tyson. One or two of the incisions are bleeding a bit, or weeping but on the whole they look pretty good.

10.00pm and going to bed. I am feeling pretty bright I had a good walk around the farm today, outside for two hours walking about. I spoke to Thomas on the phone, definitely feel much brighter. I had an email from Jane the dietician saying I have done very well on my first day's chart so I am hoping I will continue to do so. Probably felt a little hungrier tonight than I have done the rest of the time but it is four days now since I had the operation. Still on the Paracetamol and Nurofen to go to bed on so hopefully tomorrow I won't need quite so many pain killers. I do find the Paracetamol absolutely disgusting.

31st January and awake at four o'clock with a bit of pain around the port, probably over did it a little yesterday walking around the fields for a couple of hours. However, I have taken the Paracetamol, it is now five o'clock and the pain has subsided. I am feeling hungry this morning so having a cup of hot milk but needing something solid. Food never stops to dominate my thoughts just as well I have had the operation.

10.00pm and I have been hungry virtually all day today. I had the full quota of liquid I am supposed to have and also some thick beef soup throughout the day but I have still felt very hungry. I have been out in the car and that brightened me up a bit as I was feeling very, very claustrophobic just being around the house and the office all day for the last few days but my appetite has returned with a vengeance.

1st February, I have managed to sleep on my side so I am definitely becoming far more comfortable. I didn't wake up in the night for any pain killers and so everything has obviously settled down within my stomach. Much brighter this morning, feel positive about life, I haven't felt like that for a fair few days. Although I woke up feeling hungry, not ravenous like I was yesterday, I had a cup of hot milk and a teaspoon of natural Milupa honey. For breakfast I had some beef soup which sounds disgusting but rather than get hungry like I was yesterday I felt it was better to nip the hunger in the bud, and had some yogurt as well. It is now half past nine and had 100ml of hot milk again.

Going back to work today and I am looking forward to that, will be glad to get back into my old routine. All I am looking forward to doing more than anything else is walking the dogs. Jane the dietician is coming this evening so I am definitely well on the way to recovery and I feel much, much brighter in myself. Only six days have passed since I had the operation, five days is a small price to pay to change the rest of my life.

It is now ten o'clock in the evening I went to bed a little earlier tonight, around nine o'clock and have read for a while. Have been pretty tired, probably the last few days have caught up with me a bit. I have to say I have very little pain in fact I have no pain so I am not going to take my painkillers tonight. Hope I am able to sleep on my side again. So, I have made a lot of progress, had Jane the nutritionist out again this evening and she is very nice, very helpful and understanding. She understands I have a very sweet tooth and I am eating Milupa honey to satisfy that as it is pure and natural with no additives.

2nd February up with the larks this morning, I slept very badly. I have been awake since two o'clock, no pain just a dull ache where the port is so I had some hot milk, it made me feel a little drowsy and then read my book. I need to keep my mind off it, I feel a little unsettled waking up so early but now it is nine o'clock, I am out in the office and have done some work. I had Ready Brek for breakfast and a mid-morning cup of hot milk as well. I made myself a pork and cabbage soup which sounds disgusting but it was absolutely beautiful and virtually fat free. I went for a walk around the fields for half an hour this morning and I am sat in the office doing some work so definitely more or less back to a normal life.

Still getting the odd craving for something to chew and still getting the cravings for a bar of chocolate but the honey stops this, temporarily anyway. Mood swings do not seem to have appeared this morning so I am hoping I will go without them for the rest of the day. I shall be glad to be able to drive on Thursday as I hate not being able to jump in the car and just go up the shops. I feel far more relaxed today than I did this time last week, the day before the operation.

Last night I watched a little bit of Desperate Dieters on the Health Channel on Sky. There was a woman who had the banding operation the same as myself and it had gone wrong, so tonight I will watch the next episode to see what they did to correct it. I did also see them filling the port on the television so I am glad I have seen that because this has been worrying me. Apparently they numb the area with anaesthetic cream where they inject with a needle. It has been difficult to imagine that taking place but having watched it on the television in great detail I now fully understand what is going to happen when that stage comes in about another two weeks.

3rd February it is Thursday this morning and I am going to drive the car today for the first time. I am really excited about that. I have had a very good night's sleep, I slept on my side and all pain seems to have subsided. I am not sure if I am going to take the pain killers or not, I haven't had any all night and as I don't appear to have any pain at all I can't see the point in taking them but I will see how I go on as the morning progresses.

I start this morning on more solid food, to the whipped cream or apple sauce texture, also start my proper meals again so I am having a cup of hot milk to start with. I am having Ready Brek for breakfast, stewed fruit mid-morning, then thick soup for lunch and stewed apple mid-afternoon, thick soup again for dinner and hot milk before I go to bed.

2.30pm, I have been out with the dogs and still not needing any pain killers so it definitely must be healing. It is now 4.30 in the afternoon and I have been working all morning but had a disastrous lunchtime, had tomato soup which I really didn't fancy so only had 100ml also had a couple of mugs of hot milk, one in the mid-morning and one after lunch. At about 2.30/2.45pm I decided to mash or puree a proper dinner consisting of pork steak, spring greens and boiled potatoes and a little gravy I then stood and pigged straight out of the mixing bowl with a spoon. I gave myself chronic indigestion so I got my just desserts. I would say I probably ate approximately eight tablespoons straight out the mixing bowl – not to be repeated and I feel ashamed of myself for having done it. After years and years of pigging out I cannot expect my eating habits to change just like that.

I have been to Bicester, driving the car for the first time, and thoroughly enjoyed that as I missed my freedom. I felt tempted to buy chocolate as I feel really fed up with myself pigging out on the pork puree. However, managed to resist temptation and hoping I will be back on track tonight and won't eat anything else much this evening. While I was in Bicester I weighed myself - 12stone 11lbs, before the operation I was 13 stone 1lb, and that was with my boots on so you can say I have lost 4lbs.

I went to bed early tonight as I feel very tired, half past eight, probably because I have been out and about in the car, been working, walked around the fields with the dogs and eating a more solid type of food today. Also, didn't take any painkillers until going to bed.

4th February woke up at six o'clock, had a little bit of pain or ache more than pain, have taken two Paracetamol and a Nurofen. I feel a little bit moody today, it is now 6.30 in the evening and the day has been a little bit mixed. I went out in the car and managed to eat a scotch egg which I chewed thoroughly, also half an iced bun and feel totally disgusted with myself having done this. Have spoken about it to Jane the nutritionist who came this evening, she said not to feel guilty as my calorie intake is still very low, still below 1000 calories. But I do feel rotten in myself. My girlfriend Sue and her mum came to cheer me up, feel that I have let myself down. When they went I pigged a piece of cake so I am praying to God when this band is done up tight enough it will stop me doing these things. So, all in all not a very good day. The only positive thing I have done today is going for a walk up the field equating to one and a half miles.

5th February Steve has gone to the rugby and I have a day on my own today so I visited Thomas and had my first lunch out. That was a major culture shock as I thought I would be able to eat one course at least and I couldn't. I made myself feel ill, I had four mussels, half a bread roll soaked in white wine sauce from Thomas' mussels and a shepherd's pie the size of a dessert bowl - I ate a quarter of it. I feel very relieved that I couldn't eat any more and what's more I felt very ill for eating what I did. I was worried that I would still be able to pig it but I couldn't. It is my first time out to a meal, it was good because I can still pick at things and socialize but I cannot eat vast amounts thank goodness. I really enjoyed my time in London, I miss not going there. I then went to see Wendy, thought I might have a glass of wine but although it was a very good wine it tasted horrible to me and I couldn't drink it. Not that I am a great drinker anyway but normally I would have forced it down - I just didn't feel the need. Felt very tired when I got home at about eight o'clock having been out all day. I had been to the stables and it felt really good to go up there and see how Ronnie (horse) is. I am so looking forward to riding him again. I have had a very good day and thoroughly enjoyed it. I hope by the time I ride him again I will be at least a stone lighter, much better for him as he is a little thoroughbred. Best day so far. Only 10 days have passed since having the operation.

Sunday 6th February I had half a sausage for breakfast this morning with a slice of bread with no crusts, very, very soft. I also went out for lunch with George. Again, I had mussels to start with and a little ravioli but I ate a minimal amount today and I still felt full, so something is working somewhere and the weight is definitely starting to shift. I can tell by looking in the mirror, I can tell by my clothes so even if I have only lost seven or eight pounds at least it is moving. It is a week and a half since having the operation now so I am absolutely delighted with how I am feeling. Still suffering a little with mood swings, still craving sugar and I am now craving bread. Because I can't eat huge amounts it is not bothering me, I am not getting flustered over it. Definitely feel very tired again tonight, ready for a normal working day tomorrow. I did go for a long walk today though first thing this morning.

7th February and have worked all day. I have been very tired, and had a little pain in my back and my side where the pouch is. Could be because I overdid it at the weekend, also that my eating pattern hasn't been great. I have been eating too much, nothing like I used to of course, but still eating far too much and this afternoon I have done the same thing. I have trapped wind feel a little constipated and need to get back on the fruit juice following the exact diet instead of mixing it about how I feel I would like it. I am seeing Mr Appleton tomorrow so I am hoping all will be well when he sees me. My scars are disappearing; I have been rubbing Aloe Vera gel on them and they seem fainter.

8th February and woke up this morning feeling good. I have been to see Shaun Appleton today and got on very well. I had only lost 5lbs. A bit disappointing because my scales were showing 8lbs but they have never been 100 per cent accurate. He told me I am doing very well, the scars are healing nicely and the only thing I mentioned (which he hadn't told me previously) was that I had seen on the television people do suffer with hair loss after having had this operation. Not 100 per cent sure why, they think it is a lack of zinc so not unduly worried about it but I wish I had been told that before, obviously it was of little significance and if I hadn't seen it on the television I wouldn't have known anything about it. I don't intend to worry about it. I saw Jane, the nutritionist and had a good meeting with her, she always inspires me and I realise that she is going to be the key to my success.

10th February, have been for a walk, feeling good today, very much like my old self and back to normal.

15th February, have been out to dinner last night for Valentines day. I have now eaten out about four or five times since I had the operation and it has really brought home to me how much food I used to bulk down. Having the band, even though it is not inflated yet, has dramatically reduced my intake of food and what a relief, not to be able to gorge myself. A snack to me was four Frey Bentos family size steak and kidney pies one after the other and still had room for more – that was the sort of quantities I was able to eat, just sitting in the chair, eating and watching the television whilst stuffing my face. Thank God that is over and I am making good progress at eating small amounts, normal amounts, and feeling much better in myself for it. The mood swings are sorting themselves as well. The nutritionist said my system had got into a cycle of eating fatty foods high in fat and carbohydrates, no balance in my food intake whatsoever, high in sugar, and it has taken a little while to get out of my system.

21st February, I had a little discomfort today for the first time. I rang Mr Appleton who assures me that it is the stitches dissolving. Nearly four weeks since I had the operation and I will be really glad when I have the balloon pumped up on the 9th March because I am starting to feel as though I can really eat again, although I am only eating 1300 calories a day, much better than when I was eating 5000, but all the same I don't really want to be able to eat vast amounts. Roll on the 9th March.

9th March and the day has arrived where I have my balloon blown up, it is exactly six weeks since I had the operation. I am back in fighting form, feeling very fit. My appetite has resumed almost back to normal so I am very relieved I am having the balloon pumped up. I haven't had any problems really, only if I eat a bit too fast I develop chronic indigestion. Once the balloon is blown up I won't be able to eat such large amounts again. I would say I have probably lost about 10lbs since I had the operation. Roll on 4.30 this afternoon.

I have now been to see Mr Appleton and feel really depressed. I had the balloon inflated with 4.5ml and I have come home and eaten a massive portion of shepherd's pie and a yogurt and don't feel full. Something is wrong so I must ring him tomorrow.

10th March woken up feeling quite distressed at six o'clock. I am going to ring Mr Appleton first thing this morning hoping he will ring me straight back. On the 18th March Mr Appleton is going to fill the balloon to 6ml.

Friday 18th March 2005 and the day has come to have the balloon inflated for the second time as the first time insufficient fluid was used for my large appetite. Still very nervous, but roll on 12 noon. I shall be glad to have the scan to see that it is all in place.

Just come from the scan at the Shelburne Hospital and having the balloon inflated, not a very pleasant experience, but on the other hand I am very squeamish. Nothing really to worry about at all, only the thought of it, it gave a funny sensation when the balloon was being filled. Seeing it on the screen after Mr Appleton had explained it made it much clearer that all was going well. The liquid I had to swallow to make sure that it was going through properly was vile and I did manage more or less to faint a couple of times. I was stood between the scanning machine and the bed, however, after it was over I felt a little weak. I would strongly advise anybody to be driven to have this procedure and not to drive themselves. Within an hour it was all over.

I have been out this evening and could hardly eat anything but can drink liquid. I feel much better, much happier and in control again.

Saturday 19th March I have ridden four horses this morning and this afternoon I have completed a 10 mile walk around the Radnage area which is very hilly. I took a small picnic with me, I have been eating small amounts on a regular basis, things like sausages and smoked salmon sandwich, all in very small amounts and eating at a regular time about every hour having a little something. I have drunk a litre of water whilst walking the 10 miles. Although I am tired I feel good. Very relieved the band is working. I am burping a little just bringing up watery substances, the band is stopping things going through too quick and I must be still eating too quickly.

Sunday 21st March, again ridden four horses this morning and have been for an eight mile walk this afternoon with Sue. I have carried out the procedure and eaten a little but often. No real discomfort, feeling much better mentally and no mood swings. My average portion size is probably a side plate full. I can drink 600mls of water or milk quite comfortably.

Monday 22nd back to work and feel much better in myself. I have eaten more today, not a great deal more but had six small meals throughout the day. Feeling good, been dancing this evening and feel even better for having a bit of exercise after sitting in the office all day.

23rd March thought today I would cheat and have a piece of bread and butter pudding from the bakery and that made me very sick. The band definitely didn't like it so I won't be doing that again. I have eaten my six small portions and also been to see Jane the dietician. I am absolutely thrilled to learn that I have hit the stone mark, weighing in at 77.8kgs, I am very pleased. I think she was quite surprised at the amount I can still eat so the band probably needs to be a little tighter. My tummy does rumble a bit but nothing like it did when I first had the operation.

24th March have felt a little hungrier today but haven't been able to eat vast quantities, I think I could probably do with the band being a fraction tighter. I haven't had a great deal of exercise today but I am still feeling hungry.

25th March been riding, felt very hungry at lunch time, tried to eat a sardine salad and made myself very sick, didn't chew it properly, it lodged and I had to bring the whole lot back up. Have been shopping and feel much better now. Nothing like retail therapy will be glad when I can fit into my nice clothes again.

31st March I am having my band tightened tomorrow. I am not looking forward to having it tightened but I am looking forward to having the amount of food I am eating reduced. I can still manage to eat a whole pizza and also two rounds of sandwiches all on the same day this is far too much. I have been very well in myself and I know I have lost over a stone.

1st April I have been down to see Mr Appleton who was absolutely charming as always, made me feel very relaxed didn't feel half as uptight about having the band topped up today. He topped it up to 7.5ml he was originally going to add 1ml but decided to put in 1.5ml because the procedure makes me feel so sick. Not painful or uncomfortable, it is the liquid I have to swallow, so that he can see the band is working properly, tastes of aniseed and I cannot abide aniseed. It makes me feel weak and sick so he thought he would top up with a little more to save me having to go through the same procedure again too quickly. So I now have 7.5mls in there and I do feel a bit rough, still feel a bit sick and it is now 4 hours since the procedure. I wasn't well enough to go riding this afternoon but feel relieved that I have had the band re-tightened.

2nd April still don't feel right, haven't been able to eat or drink anything properly, have been very sick haven't brought up anything as I haven't eaten anything for best part of 24 hours but bringing up gas. I am hoping it will soon subside. This evening I have managed to have a cup of hot chocolate, have ridden four horses today and also completed a 12 mile walk with Sue in preparation for Peru, the Inca Trail. I feel much better and I hope it has all subsided now and I can continue to eat minimal amounts and be able to drink without being sick any longer.

3rd April woke up feeling much better this morning, I had a cup of hot milk, this has stayed down and didn't have any gas coming back up so worth persevering. I have also had a couple of pieces of dry toast and for lunch I made some home made vegetable soup and had about three tablespoons, so I am definitely in control again. The weight has dropped off me over these last few days but I expect some of that will go back on now I have started to eat again and I am getting plenty of fluid down me. I feel well in myself and I think I have persevered no matter how rough I felt. I didn't want to go back to see Mr Appleton and have to swallow any more of the dye to see if it was working or whether he wanted to take some out, I just couldn't face swallowing that liquid. It is the best deterrent from food, it is absolutely disgusting. I think I will have to remain on liquidised food for a week at least, but as long as I am able to eat something I think liquidising everything is the answer.

I am having difficulty in finding the Centurum Chewable A-Z so I have the tablet form and have to break them in half. I do find them difficult to swallow now I have had the band tightened. I am still filling in the food sheets for Jane, the nutritionist but the last few days there hasn't been much to fill in as I have been living on hot milk.

4th April and quite a sad day for me today, it would have been my late husband's birthday. I am going to have dinner with my son Thomas in London, even though I am hardly able to eat anything, but it will be interesting to see how I cope in a social situation.

I finished work at two o'clock, caught the train at three o'clock and was in London by four. Tom and I had an early dinner at Ask - his choice. Not very proud of myself, I managed to eat one whole mushroom which was stuffed with goat's cheese & breadcrumbs and the size of a large penny (that is the old penny). I also managed to eat an eighth of a pizza taking the pepperoni off (I had a slice of Thomas'). I really enjoyed it, ate it very slowly, chewed it thoroughly and didn't feel sick afterwards. I didn't drink my mineral water with it because you are not supposed to drink with your food and I was worried I might make it swell and give myself chronic indigestion. I coped well, felt comfortable and managed to hold a conversation without dominating it with what I have had done to myself. We walked down to Starbucks and had a cappuccino each, a small for me and a large for Tom, I drank that slowly and comfortably, then walked back to the station and came home, felt I had had a really good evening. I didn't have anything except a 100ml Actimel yogurt drink when I got home, so a good day for the 4th April.

5th April feel bright this morning, had 300ml of hot milk and a tablespoon of liquidised bacon, tomato and potato at 6.30 this morning as I felt quite hungry. I did cough a fair bit in the night bringing up small amounts of phlegm but nothing major so I am sure I am well on the road to recovery, although it has taken me four days since the extra 1.5ml was inserted in the pouch. I definitely feel more like my old self today. I probably feel far chirpier than Prince Charles, Camilla Parker- Bowles and Tony Blair this morning anyway!

Definitely a much better day today, have been able to eat porridge for breakfast, half a smoked salmon sandwich mid-morning, some liquidised bacon & potato soup for lunch, a dry slice of toast mid-afternoon, 100ml Actimel and for my tea I had one tablespoon of fish and mushy peas. I have only had one really bad bout of indigestion and that was after the fish and mushy peas. I finished off the evening with a cup of hot skimmed milk.

7th April and feeling completely like my old self. I have managed to eat a whole lamb chop liquidised with two tablespoons of Brussel sprouts and carrots today divided into three meals. I have eaten one and a half sausages and a yogurt, also 600ml of milk, so definitely on the mend and certainly enjoying my new found freedom of not being able to gorge. It is such a relief, I would advise anybody who has an eating disorder especially gorging to seriously look at this operation. The consequent throwing up has completely stopped and the regurgitation has virtually stopped.

8th April had a very good day, plenty of energy, rode four horses and mucked out three. Have been busy at home and been out to dinner tonight where I managed to eat a little rice, chicken korma and a tiny piece of naan bread. So, had a really good day and feel well in myself. Everything has settled down, just have to eat very slowly and chew my food properly.

12th April and I can say that I am able to eat minimal amounts properly, but I have this urge to keep gorging and as I am unable to eat it I am ending up throwing it away. It is very much a mind over matter problem and I am unable to come to terms with the fact that I can eat so little. The weight is definitely dropping off me and I think it is going to take a little longer to adjust than I first thought. I am very happy with what is happening, it is just the food factor, I didn't realise how much I was out of control of what I was eating. I keep feeling the whole time that I want to have heaps and heaps of food and I keep fancying different things to eat so I just drift from one plate of food to another and can't eat any of it. But I am sure as time goes by it will change. I am eating and drinking enough to sustain being healthy, but because my appetite was so huge beforehand I am finding it very different. One thing for sure my hip is feeling a lot better than it was due to the weight loss.

14th April had a very good day today food wise, have been able to eat more or less normally, small amounts, starting with porridge this morning, a beefburger at lunch time with half a bun and a small salad, half a smoked salmon sandwich mid-afternoon. This evening I had an ounce of steak, this doesn't sound a lot, but there is no way I could have managed steak up until now and also a 100g rice pudding. So, feeling really pleased and very well in myself tonight.

16th April, 100% fitter, feeling well, being able to eat more or less properly (by normal people's standards). I am very strong in myself, the mood swings have stopped, feeling good, the best thing I have ever done having the band fitted.

19th April I am having my first salad. I managed to eat it and kept it down so really made progress in these last few days. I feel I can almost eat anything now, just very small amounts and it feels wonderful. I need to admit that three days ago I ate a bar of Galaxy chocolate and today I have eaten a total of four sausages throughout the day. I need to change my eating habits and eat better quality food.

24th April my first holiday having lost the best part of two stone, and not looking completely like a beached whale. I do feel confident enough to walk about in my shorts, which is more than I would have done back in January. It was quite nice to fit back into a size 16 sawn off jeans instead of having to wear size 18/20.

11th May it is a beautiful sunny day and how nice it is to get out of bed and feel agile and not bulky any longer. Although I have probably only lost best part of two stone the difference in me is incredible. I feel active, very agile, full of life, healthy. For the first time ever this morning when I had my breakfast of scrambled egg on a slice of wholemeal toast, after eating half of it I knew I felt full and was able to stop. I felt in control of my eating habits - major progress. My face has lost its bloated look and I now have a waist, having gone down from 38 inches to 34 inches and I am so much fitter.

12th May another pretty good day, rode four horses and went to see Mr Walker about overseeing a building job for him and also rung a new Physio in Ludgershall – yes very positive day today.

CHAPTER 3

Adjusting Socially

13th May and I feel good this morning. I had a Weetabix for breakfast, cheese sandwich at lunchtime and saw Tony O today, he hasn't seen me for about five months and couldn't believe how well I looked. It probably helped because I had my hair cut but can't help thinking that I do look well. Went out to dinner with Mike and Julie, we had a good meal and I could eat prettily normally, not huge amounts thank goodness – the band is my friend and not an enemy!

14th May and a briefing at Hampstead today regarding the Inca Trail Walk, Sue and I went up together. They all had sandwiches with lettuce in and I am not able to eat lettuce very well so I gave those a miss rather than have a choking and coughing fit. The Inca Trail looks very exciting and I am looking forward to doing it on 29th September. It is a 10 day trip walking 5 days trekking, sleeping in a tent for 5 nights but sharing with Sue so it will be a good giggle if nothing else.

16th May and friends from Australia have arrived to stay with us for three weeks. It is so good to see them after two years. They couldn't help but say how well I looked, and of course I do, I feel quite tanned as I have just returned from Egypt so I probably look how I did when they last saw me in Australia. As I have now got my eating down to a fine art they would never know I had an operation to stop me eating. Not because I am eating vast amounts but because I am eating what people with a normal appetite would eat but it has taken quite some time to reach this stage.

17th May, Lisa called in and couldn't get over how much weight I had lost since she saw me back in January. She said how I had lost the bloated look that I had acquired and that my hips and bum look about half the size they were. So, real compliments from one of my best friends and I feel very good about it. I am looking forward to having the band tightened.

18th May and in a good routine regarding the food, Weetabix for breakfast, half a sandwich for mid-morning, light lunch of a small ham salad, a small pot of low fat rice pudding for mid-afternoon, and for evening meal the same as everyone else – possibly fish in butter sauce with salad and new potatoes, hot milk before I go to bed.

19th May – running a coffee morning this morning for Marie Curie Cancer Care and not behaving so well today, cakes are on show and I have managed to eat four – not very good. I feel very annoyed with myself that I have done so but I have been working hard. I have been on the go since six o'clock this morning and have been on my feet all day, it is now ten o'clock at night and having people stay is probably a little too much when you have other things already arranged and as nice as they are it is not the same as being able to just get on and do all your normal jobs. Looking forward to riding the horses tomorrow and having a break from the social side of things, the general pressure which makes me eat and that is not good. Cakes do not fill you up so therefore you can eat lots of them before the band kicks into action, high in calories, absolutely disgraceful and definitely do not want another day like today. It also didn't help by pouring with rain and instead of having 60 people attend the coffee morning we had 45 so we didn't take as much money as we had hoped.

20th May, rode out the horses this morning, had a long morning up at the stables, feel very fit and agile in myself, feel very proud of myself that I can ride four out and jump on and off the horses the same as the 19 year olds there, certainly don't feel my 52 years as I am not carrying the bulk like I was before. Steve has collected his mother and we are taking Barbara along with the two Aussies, Lynne & Neil tomorrow to see a show in London and very much looking forward to it.

Saturday 21st May and rode the horses at six o'clock this morning and we all left for London at 11.30am. Drove to Gerrards Cross, felt quite hungry and had hunger pains as I hadn't had any breakfast this was stupid, definitely need to have the Weetabix before I leave in the mornings but I didn't get round to it this morning. Had a hot chocolate on Marylebone Station and managed to eat about half a pizza for lunch. That was very nice as we all had pizza's and Steve finished the other half of mine. We then went to see The Lion King it was a hit with everyone so a good day was had by all. In the evening we ate at a little Italian restaurant by Marylebone Station, the food wasn't as good as it used to be but I managed to eat some pasta, did start to vomit a little bit, pasta again is something I find very difficult to digest along with lettuce. The only difference is that I like pasta and I am not so keen on lettuce but I find these two things difficult to digest.

22nd May and very glad I am going to have the belt tightened up on Wednesday as my appetite is quite large. Although I am having a lot of exercise I do feel I am still eating too much. Today I managed to eat a round and a half of smoked salmon sandwiches at lunchtime and tonight I have eaten a fillet steak with new potatoes and peas. I should only need half that amount with the sandwiches and Weetabix for breakfast. Eating far too much again!

23rd May and had a busy day in the office, always makes me hungry because I also get bored. I have eaten a low fat rice pudding, two Weetabix, a low fat cheese sandwich with Branston pickle, a piece of cake and some smoked haddock with peas and chips tonight – way, way too much!

Tuesday 24th May had dinner with George tonight after a very long day in the office. He cooked pork which didn't agree with me. I think either I tried to bolt it too quick or it wasn't cooked as thorough as I like it, but he is 77 and only ever aims to please so couldn't really say anything. Did go and vomit up what I had eaten, or most of it anyway unfortunately.

25th May and today I see Mr Appleton, very relieved about that as the band needs tightening. 4.30pm has been and gone and so has 5 o'clock and 6 o'clock, have had another ml put in the band and that is now up to 8ml. Have drunk the water and puked it up. Didn't feel too well, excused myself from seeing Jane as she was late seeing me anyway and got myself home. Very glad to get into bed and hope it is all going to settle down as I have organized a fashion show for tomorrow. Having the band pumped up is nowhere near as distressing or stressful as it used to be, Mr Appleton now gives me a little anaesthetic around the port and then injects the fluid into me, draws it out again to ensure he is in the right place and then puts the extra mil back in. It is painless and just the thought of it makes me feel funny, or a little faint, but nothing like it used to. I have got used to it, they say you get used to anything after a period of time and that saying is very true in this case, however there is no pain now. I don't think the next time I have it done I will feel half as screwed up as I used to.

26th May, not a very good day, rode the horses in the morning, didn't feel very good and had to come home. I must have been feeling really ill for me to come home and not ride two of them. Had a lie down then went on to the fashion show at Radnage with Susan at 4.30pm and felt absolutely dreadful. I collected Edna & her sister and also Shirley en-route and felt sick all the way there, when I got there I was vomiting for all I was worth I think the band must be too tight. I will try and persevere with it but I really do think it must be too tight. Vomiting over a public toilet is not my idea of fun. I was very glad when the show was finished and driving back I had to stop the car four times to vomit. I felt very dehydrated and by the time I actually dropped the others home and got in Steve took one look at me and I think he thought I was going to collapse. He put me to bed. I couldn't swallow anything, hadn't been able to drink anything and just puking all the time and feel terrible, absolutely terrible. Steve got me some ice and laid it on my forehead, I washed my face in cold water, laid down, got up, laid down, got up, just didn't know what to do with myself, felt absolutely horrendous, will definitely need to call Mr Appleton tomorrow.

27th May I phoned Mr Appleton's secretary at eight o'clock, feel absolutely dreadful and puked virtually all night, there is just nothing left, I have even been bringing bile down my nose, awful. I don't think I can ever remember feeling so ill, no call back from Jackie, have rung Jane the nutritionist but she is going on holiday, have left a message and just hope Mr Appleton gets back to me.

Yes, Mr Appleton has rung and told me to be down at Wycombe by twelve, definitely will be as I feel so lousy, absolutely lousy. Steve drove me and when Mr Appleton saw me, took all the fluid out of the band. This all stems from having the band tightened after not chewing the pork properly at George's. I am sure this trouble has caused a blockage because this morning I have vomited so much and eventually shifted a lump of pork and it was like rubber. That doesn't mean to say the band wasn't too tight, it just means that I bolt my food and there wasn't a big enough hole for it to go through. I am very relieved Mr Appleton has let the band down because it is Bank Holiday weekend, he is going way and I have guests and I cannot afford to be like I have been for the last few days all over the weekend. Now it is down I can drink and I have drunk four litres of water. I was so dehydrated and only too grateful to still be alive and here to tell the tale.

28th May, Saturday and Mr Appleton called to make sure I was alright and I am pleased to say that I am and we are having a proper family day today as we are going to see Tom and have dinner out.

30th May, Bank Holiday Monday, feel much better and have ridden the horses this morning, back to my old self and pleased to say I am not pigging out even though the band has been let down temporarily. My appetite is no where near as huge as it was so that feels very good. I haven't pigged out once over the weekend even though I probably could have but my appetite has definitely subsided so as far as I am concerned the band has been doing its job.

1st June, not feeling very good as I have a very sore throat, feel pretty grotty with it and my tongue has a thick white coating. I have ulcers in my mouth, not very good. I think when I see Mr Appleton later on today I will tell him I will not have the band tightened yet as I don't feel well enough. I have seen Dr Watt to get some antibiotics for my throat after all that vomiting, didn't expect to get away with that totally scott-free so hopefully the antibiotics will clear the infection up.

3rd June and my throat still feels absolutely terrible and we are going to a 50th Wedding Anniversary tomorrow so I am hoping I will feel better, spent most of the day in bed after riding the horses out.

4th June, rode the horses this morning, feel agile, diet is more or less back on track, not put on any weight which is even better and feel really good in my posh outfit to go to the Golden Wedding Anniversary, so nice to be back in size 14 clothes instead of wearing size 22. I have probably lost the best part of 2½ stones and it is very, very nice to be wearing smart clothes again with high heels and not feeling like an elephant, or mutton dressed as lamb. Delighted with myself even though I have a bad throat and now returned from the party. I have had a wonderful time. Everyone said how great I looked, I am vein but I really did enjoy it and Steve and I both thought we looked a million dollars so that is good. We met so many nice people, people we hadn't seen for years although Geoff sat us with people we had never met but they were all lovely, a real mixture, mainly all worked in the city and everybody else who were there were probably farmers so he felt we would have a good time with them and we certainly did.

5th June and my throat is still bad but it is definitely improving. I have ridden all the horses this morning so very active today and have done a 15 mile walk with Susan, taking in Brill Hill, Long Crendon Hill and Muswell Hill, both absolutely shattered when we finished but we did have a good laugh as always. We ate a little bit of a picnic coming back but didn't begrudge eating an ice-cream off the ice-cream van (very out of character for me because I don't normally like ice-cream) but Susan and I both felt that we deserved it. I don't think I will put on any weight having just walked 15 miles.

8th June and life is just ticking by nicely, looking forward to having the band filled a little now because the appetite is starting to return and that won't do me any good at all. I have a very busy remainder of the week as I have the nearly new bazaar and Marlow Regatta this weekend so plenty of opportunity to eat and don't want to be doing that if I can possibly avoid it.

11th June, still have the bad throat but nowhere near as bad as it was. Ran the nearly new bazaar for Marie Curie Cancer Care, had a very successful day and took just over £1,200 so delighted with that and very grateful to everybody who donated goods to us it was well worth doing.

12th June and feel very hungry this morning, throat is a little better and Marlow Regatta all day today. It is a little bit cold to be wearing flimsy clothes but had a very good day, very nice picnic and a lovely day has been had by us all. It is very nice to be out with friends for the day – all said how slim I look, I feel good. Mind I am not kidding myself I think a lot of it could be that I still haven't put back on all the fluid that I lost from the vomiting so I don't think it is all actual weight that I have lost.

14th June and have been down to The Paddocks to see Mr Appleton who has put in 6mls to start inflating the band again. Very relieved he has done so, drunk a glass of water, waited half an hour, it stayed down and feel very relieved that I had the fluid put back in. No panic while he inflated the band this time, same procedure – laid me down, anaesthetised around the port and injected into the port. It was painless, but I still cover my eyes because I can't stand the sight of needles but painless. A little aware of the sensation of the liquid going in, no pain and not distressing any longer.

15th June, Wednesday and yes I need more than 6mls in it! I still managed to eat two Weetabix this morning, did feel full afterwards so it has stopped me wanting more so I shall arrange for a further appointment to have it tightened next week.

16th June, rang The Paddocks this morning to make an appointment to see Mr Appleton next week regarding having the band tightened. I received a phone call back from Mr Appleton this evening to say that I cannot have the band tightened for two weeks as it has to have time to adjust from having the 6mls inserted, the pouch needs to settle down I suppose. I haven't had any gas this time, I feel really good and I know I can have it more inflated. I am not worried about having the procedure carried out any longer so I will make the appointment for two weeks time.

20th June, had a good week-end, eating is back to normal, I feel good in myself, the band is restricting me from over-eating even though it is not stopping me. I am very relieved it is doing its job – worth the £7,200 no question about that.

21st June and have the Duckworth's coming to dinner tonight, it will be interesting to see how I fare sitting with other people eating a meal, always a little bit worried the first time when I haven't seen people for a long time as I don't want them being over concerned because I cannot eat like I used to. I don't want three courses any longer, still can only manage 1-1½ courses which is more than enough for somebody who is four feet eleven tall.

The evening went well and the food stakes were good, didn't seem awkward at all, just had one glass of spritzer and some still water. I am ok with fizzy water but better with still water. Food wise I managed to keep everything down but was filled up pretty quick just after a main course of half a chicken breast, salad and a jacket potato. A far cry from the days of a whole chicken and a plateful of chips followed by a mixing bowl of trifle!

22nd June, have been to aerobics tonight and quite enjoyed it but didn't feel quite as active as normal, whether or not that is because the weather is pretty appalling or just because I have had quite a busy week-end and couple of days.

24th June, had my hair cut today, rode the horses and my hairdresser who I have had for some 15 years couldn't get over how well I looked and commented for the first time since I had the band fitted, six months ago, that she thought I had lost a lot of weight so it is starting to show and I am very pleased about that. Six months might sound a long time but this is a lifetime changing experience for me and I knew it wasn't going to be a five minute wonder so I am not too bothered about it taking a little time to get the weight off because I know it will stay off.

Week-end of the 25th June, horses, horses and more horses and gosh I love them and it feels so wonderful to feel agile enough to be riding them, working with them and dashing about around them, really enjoy it.

27th June, had lunch with Sandra today and she is going to have the same operation that I had with Mr Appleton, she is looking forward to it, a bit nervous just like I was, all the same fears and anxieties but I am sure she will be ok. It was good to sit there and eat sausage and mash, only manage one sausage and one tablespoonful of mash instead of managing to eat three sausages and three tablespoonfuls of mash. I have to say Sandra was very impressed but I was full up so there was no point in forcing it down – good old pub lunches.

28th June and I have had a busy day in the office. I am seeing Mr Appleton tonight to have another ½ml put into the band. It is now seven o'clock and I have had the band inflated by another ½ml - 6½mls now, it was no problem at all, just as before a little anaesthetic around the port, laid flat on my back so I can't faint and Mr Appleton putting the needle in, drawing a bit of fluid out then putting the extra half back in. We both agreed we have it down to a fine art with me now and it is so nice to know I am not going to actually faint each time I have it done.

Andrew was at home last night when I got back and he couldn't get over how good I look - god it is just getting better and better! Everyone I see now notices how well I look so I am feeling very pleased with myself, Mr Appleton and with the band. I really would like to lose another ¾ of a stone before I go to France on the 3rd August, so I am certainly going to stop eating so many sausages, cheese sandwiches and cut down the amount of spread on my bread. I have to make a concerted effort on the eating front as well as the volume of food I eat, because although the quantity of food consumed has been cut down drastically, and I am losing the weight I could do with the next few pounds coming off a little quicker and only I can make that happen but at least I know that.

30th June and I am off to ride the horses feeling very positive in myself now I have made the decision I have to change what I put into my mouth and eat. I need to concentrate on eating more greens and fruit, I do not like either very much but to speed up the weight loss I know I have to make this dramatic change in my diet as at the moment I basically live on carbohydrates with a low fat intake. The carbohydrates are making me bloated and they are also making me feel stodgy around my middle so greens, veg and fresh fruit here I come!

Although I only had ½ml inserted into the band it has made a difference, I had my two Weetabix for breakfast this morning and feel full up not needing to have a slice of toast to top it up so I make progress.

1st July today and it is about six months now since I had the operation, approximately two stones lighter and although I only have 6½mls in the band I have had a bit of a problem digesting bread today, I think I have been eating it too quick. I also had ham with the bread and I am far better with fish than I am on meat. I have to adjust what I am eating because I really am having a job to chew meat sufficiently to digest it properly so it is time to change that completely and stick to fish and soft mince type meats rather than ham and beef.

For the first time since I had the band adjusted I have brought up a little gas today but I am sure that it is because I drank water with a crusty baguette.

2nd July and today has been pretty stressful and so I have been eating for England, I have eaten 3 Galaxy cakes (the equivalent of swiss rolls), 2 crusty rolls with cheese and beetroot – didn't chew it properly and puked it up. I feel bad in myself for having had such a bad day with it. I started off alright with a couple of Weetabix, went and rode out two horses at half past seven this morning and then went selling raffle tickets for Marie Curie at the garden centre. I returned to the stables to do the horses up because Amy couldn't manage and this evening I went to Windsor Theatre. I had half a pint of cider, again not very good for the diet, really must change my eating habits or I will not be doing myself justice (or Mr Appleton for that matter). I need to speak with Jane the nutritionist as I haven't heard from her for quite a while and it is showing with my diet – not that I am blaming Jane, I am blaming myself for not abiding by the rules.

Sunday 3rd July and started the day off well by taking fruit to the stables instead of taking a stout sandwich, however, returned having not eaten the fruit so not so good. Steve cooked me a plate of vegetables today which I couldn't face so ended up eating some olives, cheese and a beefburger – not very healthy but not vast amounts either. Hopefully tomorrow will be better. Must try harder.

5th July and didn't have a very good day yesterday, ate a load of junk, sweets, cake but did have a bowl of pasta with green olives. All the rest of the day I ate sweets. Need to change dramatically. This morning I have come to the conclusion that I cannot face anything green whether it be vegetables, salad or fruit. I like things that are stodgy, how am I going to change that? Only I can do that I must try harder otherwise the weight won't come off any more than it already has. The band has stopped me gorging so I am eating much smaller amounts, probably a fifth of what I was eating but the weight loss has slowed down dramatically.

I am really looking forward to having the band tightened on the 12th July. Have weighed myself and haven't put on any weight, absolute miracle but I still feel very cross with myself.

7th July and started the day off better today. I had two Weetabix for breakfast, a banana mid-morning and dry fried bubble & squeak for lunch, with two grilled slices of bacon and one dry fried egg. Hopefully I will be good for the rest of the day. I am really struggling with it but eating a banana is a major improvement as I haven't eaten a piece of fruit for a very long time. The bubble & squeak was mainly spring greens and green beans with a couple of small boiled mashed potatoes added. I need to see Jane the nutritionist, because I haven't heard from her for a long time and I am in a position where I need the band tightened sooner rather than later, because I can't control the amount of food I am putting in my mouth. Although I am not gorging like I used to, I have probably cut down by over three quarters, I feel really fed up with myself that I am not controlling it. Even though I have been pigging out I haven't put on any weight which is a great relief. I confess last night I managed to eat a steak and kidney pie, the first one since I had the operation. I mustn't do it again, really bad, but better than before as I would have eaten three to four one after the other followed by a family size bar of chocolate! Not funny.

8th July and I have a really bad throat again, whether it was due to being sick yesterday I am not too sure. I have gargled with some scotch to take some of the pain away and at least I can swallow now. I don't know if this is all to do with the band or not but obviously being sick yesterday because I ate a sandwich too quick hasn't helped. I also did a six mile walk yesterday and felt dreadful by the time I got back so something is not right. I have started on another course of antibiotics this morning. I have also noticed my hair is falling out again so I will have to speak to Jane although I haven't heard from her I will have to ring her.

11th July and had a very busy weekend, done reasonably well food wise, managed to eat a salad last night with a steak and Weetabix for breakfast for both days. Looking forward to having the band tightened and this morning I am having a well grilled bacon sandwich with mustard and no Flora. Roll on six o'clock tomorrow and my appointment at The Paddocks. I am pleased to say I haven't put on any weight in fact I think I have lost approximately another two pounds which might not seem a lot but assuming the band isn't tight enough for me I think I have done very well. It restricts what I am eating but it isn't as tight as I need it also I know it will not stop me eating chocolate!

12th July have had the band tightened today. I was looking forward to it, it wasn't painful and has now been done. I have managed to eat some scampi and rice for my tea so I feel that it is not too tight at the moment, it is comfortable. It will stay like this for two weeks. I stayed the half an hour after Mr Appleton had given me the injection, he first of all numbed it with a little anaesthetic and then he put the needle into the pouch. No pain at all and have really made progress with this because I wasn't even nervous while he was doing it tonight. I am so much fitter and really enjoying the horses, even the hot weather isn't getting to me like it would have done if I were still carrying the excess two and a half stones I have lost. I look forward to getting another stone and a half off as soon as possible now.

14th July and had a good day yesterday except I had a little frothy gas every time I ate something because the band is that little bit tighter. Did puke three times but that was probably because I tried to eat chips, also tried to eat king prawns and bread. I can eat ordinary fish like haddock ok so at the moment the band is tight enough but I know I will need to have it tightened again in two weeks.

14th July and have done nothing but vomit all day. All I have managed to keep down is a bag of crisps, a bag of sweets and water to drink. Not very healthy, not very good diet food and need to really change what I have been eating. I was able to keep a slice of bread down, unable to keep a very well grilled beefburger down. I missed breakfast because I overslept and had to be up at the horses by 8.30am so not a good day diet wise, also the vomiting is wearing but I am sure it will improve.

15th July better start today, managed a Weetabix for breakfast and that is good wholesome food so I hope I will stick to it from now on as I can definitely see a lot of calories by eating junk with no goodness in it and keeping it down. I will have pureed home made vegetable soup for lunch which will be healthy and we will go from there. I am making a concerted effort to improve my diet.

18th July and have come to the conclusion I cannot tolerate bread, it seems to stick, makes me vomit so I am going to stop eating it, this has happened once too often now. No matter how soft or fresh the bread is my system cannot deal with it so I will go without in future. I can eat any form of dried biscuit but cannot deal with the bread. According to the scales I think the weight is starting to come off again, this is good news. Today it has taken me an hour and a half to eat a well cooked beefburger and sausage off the barbecue so the band is doing its job and I don't need it any tighter at the moment.

28th July, six months since the operation. Have noticed I am on real sparkling form. I feel very, very fit, I am riding five horses for a whole week and have realized all the flabby skin on my legs has tightened up, I feel a million dollars. My looks have returned and my hair is shining so I am feeling much, much better.

At the weekend we had some friends come for lunch and I noticed my girlfriend had put on a lot of weight. I felt so relieved this is no longer happening to me. I also noted how depressed she was about it, I did not tell her what I had had done because she is not huge by any means but she is pretty big. I was conscious not to say to her I had spent money on cosmetic surgery to stop myself getting fat. Although, I am very proud of myself at having the operation, it was a very positive step. I no longer appear to hear from the nutritionist so maybe she only speaks to and sees us for the first three or four months, it is now exactly six months ago since I had the operation.

3rd August today and going on holiday to Biarritz in France, feel really good in myself, I am fit, have lost a lot of weight and my face has a youthful look about it again even though I am 52 and can't disguise that fact. I feel very good about my whole well being. I could probably do with the band being tightened to 7½ml but decided not to so I can eat some solid food such as crusty bread while I am away as I much prefer bread and cheese. I can't eat huge amounts, only little bits but that is better than not being able to eat any. The puking has completely stopped and I have learned what I can and can't eat. Red meat is a definite no go, miss my fillet steaks but not the end of the world, not to be fairly slim and fit.

I am ready for the holiday, have been working very hard with the horses, have done a whole week mucking out eight and riding four each day - I shall be glad of the rest. Put a bottle of water and a little packet of Go-ahead snacks in my bag because I do need to snack quite regularly although the amounts I eat are fairly small. To really make my day I have managed to get dressed in my size 12 jeans – wonderful. They are a fraction tight around the waist but nice around the arse!

7th August and have just returned from Biarritz. Had a wonderful time, it was so good to be able to put on a swimsuit and have it fit comfortably, also to be able to wear nice clothes, a little Max-Mara skirt and top and Prada shoes, without feeling like a fairy elephant in them. It felt so good to be back among the normal looking, well-being people again instead of a space hopper (top heavy and little legs!).

Still unable to eat much bread or red meat but have eaten fish and basically anything light. Salads I still find difficult to digest but have eaten well while I have been away. I have eaten rice, pasta, one steak(but it took me a long time). I prefer to eat rice and fish dishes which can only be a good thing health wise. Great to be walking about in shorts and not having my legs rub together. It is great to be able to wear little t-shirts again with my arms not bulging out. Fantastic to be able to wear strappy shoes without flesh being pinched by the straps. No doubt about it the exercise has contributed tremendously towards my well being. Although I was very tired when I left on the 3rd August from all the horse riding and general stable work it was well worth the effort just to feel good within myself.

21st August it is a beautiful sunny day, I have ridden two horses and had a sun bathe in the garden with Tom, who is coming to the end of his holiday period, we had a lovely barbecue this afternoon. I managed to eat a beef burger (well grilled on the barbecue), two charcoaled sausages, one jacket potato, a tablespoonful of sweetcorn, two teaspoons of coleslaw and 1½ozs grated cheese and I thoroughly enjoyed it. It took me nearly two hours to eat it all but I have enjoyed it. I also had two glasses of red wine and a glass of water so a good day has been had by all.

23rd August today I am having the band filled with another ½ml. It is a beautiful sunny day but I am very nervous, not looking forward to it and haven't been for a good four weeks. Decided to eat my dinner before I go to my appointment at six o'clock. I had my evening meal at four o'clock in case I can't eat anything after the procedure. Sounds a bit potty but can't bear the thought of feeling hungry so I have eaten a stir-fry, nothing major or naughty just a prawn stir-fry with a few noodles.

It is now 7.30 in the evening and I have returned from The Paddocks Hospital. It was good to see Shaun Appleton who was in excellent spirits having returned from holiday, the same as myself. I was very nervous, but like I explained to him, even though I haven't lost a great deal more weight in the last four weeks since I saw him last, I feel well in myself and very fit, I have gone down four dress sizes from a size 20 to a 14. I feel that is pretty good and I am very happy with myself. When he found the port he told me it had moved this made me feel a bit strange, I don't know why it made me feel this way but it did. I should have said to him I felt as though it was a bit bruised, I could have moved it where I have been sliding down off the horses thinking about it – should have said that at the time but didn't. I felt a little funny when he injected me but it didn't hurt in any way, I just felt slightly faint and had to do some deep breathing. He was trying to joke with me but I really couldn't joke back I felt awful while having it done. But once it was over I stood up and felt fine, drank a small cup of water, could feel it lodge and then drain down with a gurgling sensation which gave me a little gas or a repeat, but I didn't feel sick so it was obviously not too tight and will stop me eating quite as much as I have been doing. I have had a glass of milk since arriving home and that has gone down fine as well. Again, a little bit of gas but nothing else. Hopefully I will only be able to manage one Weetabix in the morning, half a sandwich at lunchtime and a small evening meal instead of two Weetabix, one and a half sandwiches and quite a large evening meal. So, next step forward, next stage and hopefully the weight loss will increase a little faster.

26th August and I am having a job to eat anything solid, can manage a Weetabix and can drink milk. I have managed to eat a Go-ahead low calorie biscuit but the band is plenty tight enough at the moment. I am comfortable with it but I would not want it any tighter at this moment in time. I am full of energy, riding all the horses, doing plenty of walking, on the go all the time so my energy levels have not dropped even though I am not able to eat as much as before.

27th August it is now three days since I had the band tightened. I haven't really been able to eat much today. I managed one ham sandwich and kept it down, everything else I have puked up. Last night I went out to dinner for the first time since having it tightened to the 7½mls and was unable to keep anything down at all. I had paté to start (didn't eat the bread), followed by steak & kidney pie which probably wasn't the best choice but it had mashed potato with it and I thought I might be able to keep the potato and the gravy down with a little bit of the pastry – No – the stomach wasn't having any of it, I didn't even have a coffee. I managed a white wine spritzer but even brought that up so – so far not so good but I will persevere. I feel bright and can keep plenty of fluid down including milk, water and juice so I won't starve and I know it will get better as long as I persevere.

29th August have been out to dinner tonight, finding the band is plenty tight enough, unable to eat properly, had a couple of mouthfuls of soup and that was fine then tried a chicken breast with asparagus in sauce with nothing else but couldn't keep that down so I am eating minimal. I can manage one or two of my Go-ahead yogurt biscuits but that is about all along with water or milk. I seem to be able to drink as much as I want (100% skimmed milk that is). I have been unable to drink alcohol except the odd spritzer, very different to a bottle 4 nights a week!

30th August and another beautiful bright sunny morning today. I have been to the horses and worked up a real appetite I managed to eat half a scrambled egg. It feels as if it is going to stay down so fingers crossed it will. Over the Bank Holiday week-end I went shopping for Thomas' graduation and I have to say it was simply wonderful to buy a size 12 skirt in Hobbs and a size 14 jacket in Jaeger, both looked a million dollars and I will look like a film star at his graduation so thank you band, thank you for all your assistance.

31st August it is Thomas' graduation, have to say look 100% the proud mum dressed in my very flash outfit. He is very proud of me and told me that he loved me very much and really appreciates me looking a million dollars for him on his special day. I must be the proudest mum here today, it is absolutely wonderful, what a lovely son I have.

Today is Sunday 4th September and I have ridden out three horses, have worked very hard the last couple of days and I am very tired. We are going out for Sunday lunch today to George & Heather's. I am not over looking forward to it because I know I am going to have to eat roast beef and Yorkshire pudding but we will see how we go. It is now five o'clock in the evening and it has been a horrendous lunch, I couldn't digest any of it, as much as I chewed, as much as I mashed it into the gravy and as much as I tried I could not eat a Sunday roast in any shape or form. I apologised profusely to them and said I wasn't feeling very well. In future I shall have to re-think the roast Sunday lunches as there is no way I can cope with them. Came home and ate mince and mashed potato but having left the table eight times in a period of two and a half hours I came away feeling absolutely dreadful. There is no way I could do that to anybody again so I really do need to re-think that situation.

5th September have tried to eat a bacon sandwich this morning – fatal – could not digest it at all, really fancied it, just smelt the bacon cooking and had to have one then puked the whole lot up. I wish to goodness I had never tried so hopefully I will not try that again. I can't understand why I am not losing more weight when I am being so sick, the scales are showing that I haven't lost anything. Could be something to do with all the sweets I am eating, the fruit allsorts for instance – solid sugar! Every time I am sick, no matter where I am whether it is in a public toilet, in the bathroom in somebody's house or whatever I make sure I take my t-shirt or blouse or top half garment off in order to make sure I do not have any tell-tale signs from splashing. This really is quite a problem as when I am sick it is with gusto. Hopefully it won't be too long before I manage to stop it or just literally eat pureed food. I thought I would have learnt my lesson by now.

9th September and the eating today appears to have improved, although I did puke up half a sandwich this morning. We have been out to dinner tonight, I managed to eat a little pâté, half a slice of toast and some scampi Provencal with a little rice followed by an Irish coffee – very enjoyable – all of which has stayed down and I feel good about that. It is really good to be stood here in quality clothes, well fitting tight black trousers and t-shirt. I have had a lot of compliments tonight, it has also been the Marie Curie raffle draw and no end of people have given donations even though they had not bought raffle tickets so feel really good about myself tonight. We raised over £2,000 on the raffle and £500 of that has come in the form of donations from people in the restaurant – thank you very much to all those who have donated and to Gerry for putting up the prize money for the raffle.

I had a pretty stressful week-end with the band, Sunday in particular which was the 11th September. I found it very difficult to eat, in fact I haven't been able to eat anything and keep it down except for chocolate – not very good but at least I kept it down. I have managed to drink milk and as long as I can drink milk and water & eat chocolate I am perfectly happy, although it is not very good for my overall diet. I am now about to go away for a week to Ireland with the horses and hoping I will be alright. Time will tell and I am not going to panic about it but would like to be able to keep something down. I am sure I would be able to keep a drop of soup or something similar down.

The weight loss has definitely slowed right down even though I am not eating hardly anything it must be because I am still eating sweets.

13th September at two o'clock in the morning and I am leaving in a horse box with my friends Bumble and Amy for

Necarne Castle in Northern Ireland. We have three horses on board and a heap of food. I am hoping I will be able to eat some of it without puking – bit like going back to my misspent youth. We are away for a week and I am really quite excited about it especially as I am sure with a bit of luck we have the winner on board. Today I have managed to keep down mince & mashed potato and a few Go-ahead biscuits. During the journey I ate a packet of cheese & onion crisps and a bar of chocolate. Diet food I don't think so!

Having arrived on the 14th of September the place is magnificent and the castle is fantastically stunning. Our stables are beautiful and the horses have settled in well. We do have a long way to walk from the lorry to the stables but that is really good as it is up hill coming back from the stables. As I will always be laden with tack, feed buckets or hay nets etc. it will be good practice for Peru where I am going in a fortnight's time to trek for six days, sleeping five nights in a tent. Not looking forward to that bit but having now had my first night in the horse box and nearly froze to death I have learned I need to buy a sleeping bag. It is so important to exercise even though I have the band fitted and I am really appreciating this extra exercise walking backwards and forwards to the stables, must be half a mile each way. I reckon throughout the day I am walking about 14 to 15 miles.

Saturday 17th September and it is cross country day. We are in the lead as I speak with Moley (one of my favourites). My job today has been to lead Spicey around until it is her turn she is a little grey mare full of life and who continually stands on her hind legs. Good job I have lost weight and fit because there is no way I would have hung on to her before. So feeling very pleased with my progress and delighted we are in the lead.

Had a few drinks tonight, will probably feel terrible tomorrow as cheap wine does not agree with me. "Five star mum" is what my son calls me and five star mum I definitely am, but I will have won my £50 bet because I will have stayed in the horse box for 7 nights and neither Steve nor Thomas thought I would – just shows how well they know me! Once determined no-one could ever make me do anything I didn't want to do. The band was one thing I wanted fitted and my best friend Lisa really didn't want me to have it, but I went ahead because it was something that I truly wanted to do. Very pleased I took the plunge.

18th September fantastic we have won. As a team we feel we have won easily and how great it is to stand and have my photograph taken with Bumble, who rode the horses, the horses and their owners and the other little groom Amy, all of whom are long and skinny and I do not feel out of place stood alongside them with my new found figure (or my old figure starting to return should I say).

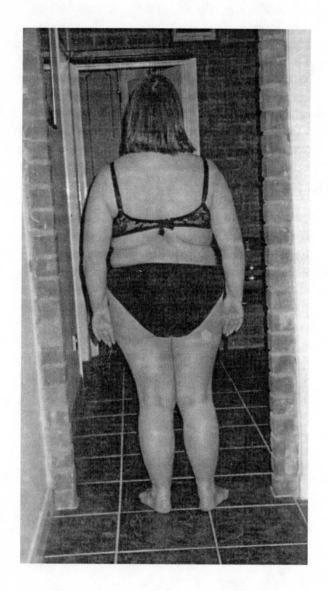

Before

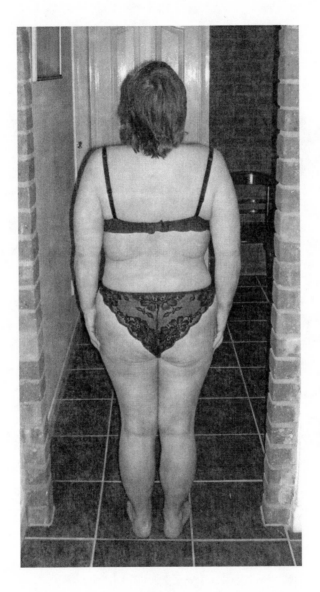

After

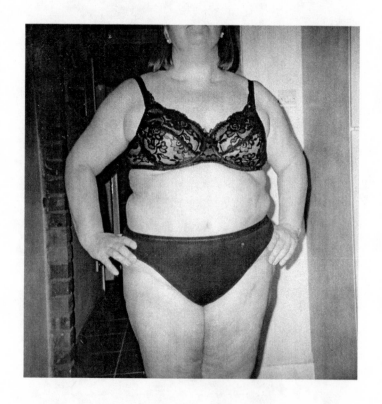

Before – Depressed and Obese

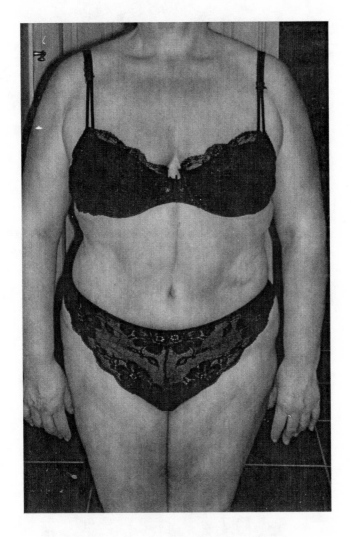

After 2 Years with my Silent Friend Fitted –
Healthy and Trim

Before – depressed and obese

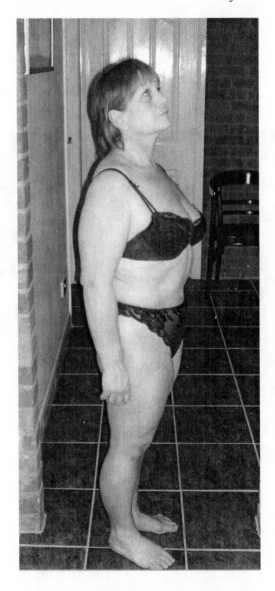

After 2 years with my silent friend fitted –
healthy and trim

*At my best friend's wedding looking like a brown couch
potato*

After my silent friend fitted – fantastically fit riding Plessy'

Healthy, trim and fit 3 years on

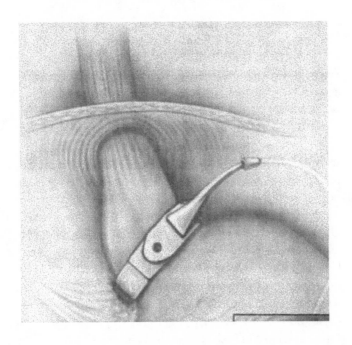

The Gastric Band

CHAPTER 4

The Inca Trail

Back home the 25th September my last walk with Sue before we go to Peru to walk the Inca Trail. I have thoroughly enjoyed our last walk completing 15 miles and found it very easy, not an inch of pain anywhere. I am certainly fit if nothing else.

Anyone reading this diary needs to know that exercise and self motivation are a major part of good self esteem, and the band alone is not enough, especially if you like things you are not supposed to eat like cheese & onion crisps and chocolate bars. So every time I eat one of these items I know I have to do more exercise otherwise the weight loss will slow down. I have muscled and tightened up tremendously, and the weight loss probably isn't as great as it should have been, but I feel very fit and my measurements are as follows – bust 39", waist 32½", widest part 37½", hips 37½", left thigh 21½", right thigh 20½", right knee 13", left arm 13", right arm 13", total loss 7" since June. Total loss of inches since the band was fitted 36½" that is just over 3ft or a yard! My skirt size is 10-12, shirt/t-shirt size 12-14 – wonderful – absolutely wonderful. Not too sure about what the scales will say, don't really care as I feel very, very good in myself – fantastic – thank you Mr Appleton.

29th September and four o'clock in the morning. I am about to leave for Peru after collecting my friend Susan, who no doubt will be a complete and utter bundle of nerves worrying herself to death that I am going to be late, but I won't be not on this occasion. I am looking forward to this now as I feel very fit and even though I still find it difficult to eat bread etc. my appetite has subsided tremendously, I can live on mince and mashed potato (both fat free of course) if need be. My special treats and my passion or obsession in life which ever you prefer to call it is still chocolate, cheese & onion crisps and also fruit allsorts, however I do try to limit these and I am sure I will have a hell of a job to buy any of these three things on the Inca Trail in Peru. Let's hope so anyway! I look forward to returning with a weight loss so that when I am next weighed by Mr Appleton I will be at least 6 or 7lbs lighter than the last time I saw him.

Susan was bright as a button and ready to go so we set off for the airport. Our first hiccup was Susan needing to get something out of her bag and couldn't remember the padlock number so we had a fit of the giggles. We met all the Marie Curie people as we arrived, the rest of the group were easy enough to pick out, all stood there in their Marie Curie t-shirts and name tags, needless to say Susan and I did not have ours on.

The flight and food were good, had a slight problem with the videos because if you pressed English it played in Spanish and vice versa but once you conquered that it was pretty good. I watched Alfie, hilarious and The Interpreter with Nicole Kidman, brilliant.

When we arrived at Lima we had been travelling for 23 hours in total. It is rather like Cuba here very third world. The hotel we are staying in (The Plaza), clean a little basic perhaps but very clean. Very relieved to find I have organized myself well enough to be able to find the things I need for tonight. I do feel tired but am going to have a drink with the group, have something to eat then to bed.

Food wise have managed to eat reasonably well today, bits & pieces on the plane, all stayed down so far. Had one piece of a club sandwich this didn't agree with me so will see how we get on this evening. Have eaten a bag of cheese & onion crisps from my suitcase, there's a surprise, they weren't even crushed in the transition from airport to airport, also a packet of fruit allsorts, very good, very healthy Mr Appleton I am sure you will be delighted to read this.

30th September the time in Lima is 3.30 in the morning, washed, showered and packed, how about that for efficiency!

5.30 in the morning local time the place is absolutely beautiful, stunning, rolling hills, lovely little square we have stopped to have a coffee before we go to our hotel, the sun is shining. The people are in local dress and have to be seen to be believed. It is rather like being in Switzerland but without the snow, everywhere is amazingly clean.

Have disinfected the door handles and bathroom taps, might be obsessed by cleanliness but do not want diarrhoea. The two main things to watch out for are gastroenteritis and altitude sickness. Won't be having either of those unless absolutely got to! Have been shopping around the markets today, bought 12 beautiful Alpaca scarves averaging approximately £2.50 each, a bargain. I went to the internet café to get addresses for the postcards, also bought the postcards and stamps today. Sue unfortunately has a touch of altitude sickness. Noticed how small the people are here they make me feel ten feet tall. Had a superb lunch, now about to go out to dinner.

1st October Saturday morning it is now 7.00am in Peru. I am sat in the open square beautiful surroundings with a fountain and the locals going to work. They are lovely people not only are they very small, they all look the same always smiling and cheerful. This area is really pretty the flower beds are beautifully planted although it is a third world country the standards are very high. Our hotel room is basic but it is clean. Last night a few of us went out to dinner, Susan unfortunately has been too ill to join in, she is suffering this morning. She has been sat up all night, had the doctor in to her and we will wait to see how she goes. It isn't looking very hopeful she will be able to complete the trail as I speak here at the moment.

Food wise I only vomited twice yesterday, once after half an avocado pear, once after I had eaten a potato which was spicy and not quite to my taste. I don't think it was the band that caused the vomiting I think it was more the taste. I am looking forward to breakfast this morning and pretty sure I shall keep that down. The altitude has made me very hungry so I have been eating low calorie yogurt bars, hopefully I won't put on any weight, but on the other hand I will have enough energy to do the walk.

I am excited this evening we are going off tomorrow morning heading towards the Inca Trail. Went out to dinner unfortunately it wasn't very hygienic there. It was probably the worst meal we have had. I tried the soup but promptly threw up - the band didn't like it - it did taste alright but it didn't suit me. So, I shall look forward to having a bag of crisps when I get back to the room.

Sunday 2nd October Susan and I have been awake since four o'clock this morning, the youngsters all came in around 2.30am and woke us up. I never got back to sleep and by four o'clock Sue and I were in full flow having a conversation. Five o'clock went down to get us both a cup of hot chocolate. I also ate two cookies I was absolutely ravenous as I hadn't kept any dinner down from last night.

We drove in the coach this morning for approximately an hour and a half from the hotel to the salt plains. When we left the coach we walked for two hours to the Sacred Valley where the salt plains are, the scenery was spectacular. It was all downhill great to start off the walking. We walked solidly for two hours and it was very hot. The scenery reminds me rather of New Zealand in a strange sort of way, maybe not quite as picturesque as New Zealand but has a similar sort of feel with the mountainous range all the way around us.

Bought a bar of chocolate when we reached the salt plains, what I didn't realise was we would have to walk along this narrow ledge really high up for approximately ¾ mile, had a panic attack. Fortunately Susan was only about six feet in front of me I did manage to call her but froze on the spot. I couldn't remember my normal phrase I need to repeat over and over again when I have a panic like this over heights - it is "nothing is as bad as you first think it is". I said this over and over again out loud (fortunately I had told Susan this the night before and she could remember it). I repeated it like a parrot for the whole ¾ mile goodness was I glad to keep moving. Susan leant me a stick, I don't know whether it helped or not, but I managed. I didn't think I was going to, so achieved something today. Not keen on the picnic lunches, everyone said how good they were but they didn't appeal to me. I managed to throw up a bread roll, a piece of cucumber and a piece of cheese. It didn't help that a flea ridden dog came and sat by my feet on two occasions. The group we are with are great fun I am thoroughly enjoying it.

Have arrived at the Libertador Hotel, Tambo Del Inca it is a three star hotel. The shower is grubby but the rest of it is not too bad. Very glad I packed my backpacker sandals cannot abide my feet on anything mucky. One very interesting thing we did see today was how the locals weave the throw-over covers and how they dye the wool etc. We also walked round another market, saw all their worldly goods. The highlight of that part of today's little trip for me was the locals drinking their homemade beer made from corn. Surprisingly it is mainly women who drink it. We saw three Europeans having a glass, you can bet your life they are all ill in bed tonight as we have been told not to drink anything that could possibly have been washed or mixed with water.

All off out for a meal tonight so I am sure we will have a good time. I am relieved the path of the Inca Trail is not terribly narrow as the panic attack has shaken me up. I am hoping I will not experience any more on this trip.

3rd October had a fantastic day, left the hotel, managed to keep my breakfast of a roll down. At ten past six this morning collected Sue & myself a cup of hot chocolate after a good night's sleep. I had a wonderful day, we walked for two hours this morning along a very narrow path I managed to be fine. On the way to the Inca Trail we stopped at an Inca village. We saw how they lived, not for me I have to say, and where they bred guinea pigs (they breed and live with them in the house), everybody is selling something but at least they don't pester you by begging to the point of where it is unbearable, they just want to sell their wares.

Walked at a good pace today, thoroughly enjoyed it. I walked at my own pace with the front group. Mainly on my own not really talking to anybody, reflected on everything going on around me, what had gone on before and after. Unfortunately when we stopped for lunch I couldn't keep my food down, managed to vomit twice, unsuccessfully attempted to eat a bread roll with peanut butter, also tried some avocado on a piece of bread but couldn't keep that down either.

Sue has been good today she appears to have felt a lot better, walked at her own pace. Sue had two sticks I had one I purchased from the Inca village. The terrain has been steep in parts but not unbearable by any means. This afternoon we walked for a further two hours (approximately 12 kilometres) doesn't sound very far in total but due to the high altitude it has been far enough. Feel in good shape, glad I have lost so much weight otherwise I would be struggling. When we appeared half way down the mountain you could see the camp site, it was a most welcoming sight it looked very neat and tidy. It is a third world country things are pretty poor out here in the mountains.

Established our tent and managed to organize ourselves. Had a strip wash, very glad that neither Sue nor I are very big because there isn't a lot of room in here although it is plenty long enough for the both of us. We managed quite well, everything is neat and tidy so far so good. I forgot to say that along the whole of the Inca trail we walked today we had a beautiful view of a very fast flowing river. We saw people fishing for fresh trout it looked pretty deep, I imagine in the rainy season it becomes exceptionally dangerous.

On our final night the 8th October I received an award and a medal for my fitness achievement. Most memorable moment of the trip apart from the fantastic scenery was a whole guinea pig stood up on the plate decorated with chips and lettuce being dished up as this is a delicacy here. Sue is vegetarian and went green! On this occasion I didn't need any help from the band to feel sick!

9th October my son's 25th birthday, I am sat at the airport just reflecting on what I have done for the last few days. If I hadn't lost all the weight there is no way I could have succeeded in this trip. The Inca trail was incredibly steep, the views have been magnificent and the people varied but really pleasant. Susan, my friend who undertook this trip with me has been ill most of the time however I think she is pleased she completed it.

Eating wise (as this diary is really for Shaun Appleton and any research he may be carrying out on the band) I have not been able to eat very well mainly because of the hygiene aspect. I couldn't face the dirty plates, knives and forks, the porters have been so grubby it put me off the food. I have been sick quite a lot from anything I have eaten although I think that is not down to the band but because of the hygiene. I have eaten lots of yogurt bars they have stayed down. I drank hot chocolate, this I brought with me although I did use the boiled water. I also drank lots of water throughout the trip. I walked in the front all the way, no-one could get over how fit I am. I have really enjoyed the hiking I can't tell you how much I enjoyed stretching out and walking at great speed in the front with the twenty year olds feeling exuberant about it. Thomas met me at the airport and he couldn't believe how well I look.

10th October back at my desk, it was good to have a night in my own bed after sleeping in a tent for five nights jet lag has kicked in good and proper. Very pleasant to eat a warm Weetabix this morning, some mashed potato with bacon pieces in with a little milk to soften it up. I have kept it all down. For tea had one smoked salmon sandwich – all remained down – wonderful after having had ten days of more or less sheer vomiting on the trek.

11th October, Dawn my girlfriend has arrived, we have been out this evening, managed to eat shepherds pie with gravy which Steve prepared for me, wonderful, really enjoyed it and kept it down. Feel good in myself, the jet lag is a little overpowering but the band must have gone back to its normal size I think the altitude must have affected it.

13th October back with the horses on full form have ridden out 4 this morning. Had a grated cheese sandwich (not able to eat the crusts) some milk and a yogurt bar. For lunch I had mince & onions, no fat, all cooked and ready for me when I came in. It is a great help having food to hand as soon as I finish the hard work because I am always starving hungry and have a tendency to bolt my food. If I haven't got to prepare my food only microwave it I find it much easier to digest and take my time eating it.

16th October having Sunday lunch at The Bull & Butcher, given up trying to eat roast beef & Yorkshire pudding, can cope with a chicken breast with gravy and mashed potato. Managed to eat half of it and feel really good, kept the whole lot down, had two white wine spritzers and an Irish coffee absolute luxury after Peru.

20th October at the stables all day, took my breakfast with me couple of yogurt bars and a grated cheese sandwich. Have eaten all of it and kept it down, took a third of a pint of fully skimmed milk and rode five horses. Have done afternoon stables, thoroughly exhausted, looking forward to having something hot when I get in. Now home, showered and clean, have eaten mashed potato with bacon bits and baked beans with melted cheese, the whole lot equating to approximately three tablespoons. I have been eating a lot of Bertolli spread to help the bread go down. I have been having extra gravy on shepherd's pie and chicken, sauce on fish, if I eat rice I always have plenty of soy sauce on it because I find trying to eat anything dry tends to stick and give me indigestion.

Out to dinner on 21st October with a group of friends, first time since I have been back, slightly nervous I won't be able to keep the food down and have to keep excusing myself from the table but I know if I eat sensibly I will be ok. The evening has gone very well, I had paté on toast to start with, a Dover Sole for my main course and an Irish coffee afterwards, two white wine spritzers, also a glass of champagne.

28th October and Steve is away for three days so no doubt I shall be eating a lot of things I shouldn't be. I had a wonderful hot chocolate to drink this morning, I have a bag of fruit allsorts to take to the stables with me and two packets of cheese & onion crisps, all very unhealthy but I know I will not be puking them up so it is even naughtier they will remain down and make me fat. Lessons to be learned by anybody reading this do not copy me with my eating habits as soon as my husband's back is turned. Now home absolutely starving at 5.30pm, had mince, mashed potato real good tip for anybody Aunt Bessie's individual portion size mashed potato is wonderful, you just heat it for two minutes in the microwave along with whatever else you are having. I need four if I am really hungry and two if I am semi-hungry. I have learnt it is easier to eat standing up, I tend to eat my food stood either at the breakfast bar and move around doing other things at the same time or when I am at the stables I eat stood up while I am tacking up a horse ready to go out riding. I find it more difficult to eat sat down at the table at normal chair height. It is not a problem at home because I can stand up but to eat out it is a bit of a problem because I have to sit at the table along with everybody else. It is whilst sat down trying to eat I seem to have more problems with puking, however whilst in Peru I am sure I was sick a lot of the time because of the high altitude and the band had tightened not because I was sitting or standing although the food was at an appalling standard anyway. However, I was advised before I did the

Peru trip that the band would tighten at high altitude by Mr Appleton.

1st November oh no dentist! I have to take Valium, always makes me starving hungry, worried to death I will be sick in Steve's car, have managed to eat a piece of fish afterwards and only sick once when I got back, not sure if it was the Valium or the fish so let's say that's the end of the first of November. I must add that the fish came from the fish & chip shop so it was deep fried in batter, very unhealthy and inundated with salt & vinegar, along with the cheese & onion crisps and fruit allsorts it doesn't sound very good but all I can say is that I don't really do this that often – honestly.

3rd November, went to have my hair cut and my hairdresser couldn't get over how much weight I suddenly appear to have lost. She hasn't seen me for six weeks I did explain to her that I am fit but have not told her I had the band fitted. She was very impressed at how trim I am looking so thank you Mr Appleton.

4th November, David my accountant came today, he was absolutely speechless when he saw how I had shrunk and that made me feel really good so no more sweets or crisps for a few weeks if I can possibly manage it and feeling really good – size 14 top, size 12 jeans, keep telling myself that I am never going to be any bigger than that ever again.

7th November out to lunch with a girlfriend Jan, her 55th birthday and going to The White Hart, not looking forward to this in case I cannot keep anything down. However, had the mushroom soup to start with it filled me up, followed by shepherd's pie for my main course, ate half of it, was worried that I would have to leave the table, did excuse myself once but just had a glass of water, couldn't even have a glass of wine with her to celebrate her birthday in case it triggered me off needing to go to the bathroom throughout the lunch. I had a cup of hot milk for my dinner because I still felt full from lunchtime, my appetite has shrunk.

10th November, Steve and I fly out to Johannesburg today, leaving Steve in Johannesburg and myself flying on to Cape Town. Staying in very nice accommodation so I can cook and please myself until Thomas and Steve join me in three days. Had a swim in the freezing cold pool, sat in the sun with two sarongs on because I am so cold and now eating baked beans and grated cheese with a small piece of toast, that is my lunch and for dinner I am having a grated cheese sandwich with a little pickle, cut the crusts off but only managed half a sandwich a cup of hot chocolate and a white wine spritzer. Had a good day but looking forward to the other two joining me, certainly not very impressed with my own company for long periods of time although I have only had ¾ of a day today on my own.

12th November Steve and Thomas have arrived this afternoon, I am pleased to see them both, we are off out to dinner. The coastline is fantastic, had a good drive around, they brought the car with them. We have been out and about around the whole area of Hout Bay and out to dinner. Didn't have much success, I chose a white fish that wasn't fine, too chunky for me and had to leave the table on four occasions, thank goodness Thomas fully understands the situation and Steve has got used to it otherwise I would have been very embarrassed. Because I hadn't eaten a great deal the day before and nothing in the morning I had tried to eat too fast, I keep doing this even after almost 12 months, I would have thought I had learned my lesson by now. I am a lot better but I still have a long way to go from the point of bolting my food.

17th November I had a wonderful time in Cape Town, South Africa. We did lots of things, had many meals out, I tried to eat things that I can digest easily, managed about a ¼ of a fillet steak, this I chewed and chewed and chewed and thoroughly enjoyed. Fillet steak used to be my passion before I had the band fitted but cannot cope with it now. I have to stick to chicken and soft fish such as Dover sole, minced beef along with cheese, paté, mushrooms and soup so still have a wide variety I can eat whilst out.

We have been to Table Top Mountain, to Cape Point where we walked right down to the point itself and back up, felt very fit, I couldn't have done that two years ago and I probably couldn't have done it a year ago due to the amount of excess weight I was carrying and the bad hip I had developed due to the extra weight. The hip has been so much better since losing the weight. We took a helicopter trip along the coastline and thank goodness I have lost so much weight otherwise I wouldn't have fitted onto the tiny seat I had to sit on, very embarrassing. So my arse is no longer as big as a barge as Steve would say. Although the weather was warm it was still a little too cold for shorts.

21st November Thomas has left for the USA today and Steve and I are now home. It is very nice to be back on my normal diet of Weetabix in the morning, some form of sandwich at lunchtime and either shepherd's pie with lots of gravy, mince and onions, mashed potato or cod in butter sauce or something similar. It is half a portion of cod in butter sauce with a quarter of a tin of mushy peas tonight.

22nd November, I feel very upset that Thomas has gone away also stressed because his flat has been sold, I have been left to deal with it in his absence. As I am stressed I bought a couple of packets of cheese & onion crisps this morning, very bad start to the day but feel full up. Had a cheese sandwich I put some of the crisps into this, also managed to eat one Weetabix. For dinner I ate mashed potato with bacon pieces and baked beans equating to approximately 4 tablespoons. It just proves that as soon as I am stressed food is the first thing I turn to, the great thing is the band will only allow me to eat a certain amount and nothing like I could before. I confess I have eaten one bar of Galaxy chocolate tonight. Steve bought me this because he knew what a state I had been in all day, hassled to death but no excuse for eating chocolate, I will try not to do it again for a couple of weeks at least.

26th November and busy with the horses, eating has been good up to now, I am very fit. Need to start the walking again as we are going to the Everest Base Camp in March. Exercise is such a major part of this, my skin is not hanging in baggy loose sacks like I thought it would (it did look as though it might to start with). The exercise has kept me tight and fit and my skin has remained quite taut and toned. Exercise is a must.

28th November out to lunch for my best friend's birthday, real celebration, not for her perhaps as she is 65 today. Strange thing, we went to lunch at a restaurant in Amersham, saw some people I hadn't seen for 20 years, had a boozy lunch and thankfully Tara, Wendy's daughter was driving. The food managed to stay down, I chose very wisely, had a small bowl of soup to start with and a potato & vegetable paté for my main course, didn't have any afters. I felt full up and didn't want to be leaving the table today. No dinner full up, my appetite has truly shrunk at last.

4th December D-Day, my own birthday, 53 how grim is that? The only good news is I am 2¾ stones lighter than I was on my 52nd birthday so I have something to celebrate. What a wonderful birthday, I rode my two favourite horses to build up an appetite for our evening meal, also did a 9 mile walk around Muswell Hill. 100% fit, couldn't feel better for my 53rd birthday even though disappointed about the years gone by and having to say that I am 53 but I only look 45 ha ha ha! Only on a good day as Steve says when there is a power cut! Ate out and that was quite successful probably because I was so hungry from the walk. I had paté to start with (no toast) and half a breast of chicken with gravy, mashed potato and green vegetables, the equivalent of approximately 4 tablespoons altogether, an Irish coffee and a couple of white wine spritzers.

Appear to eat and drink more or less the same things, but I am a creature of habit and I know they do not upset my system so I am more than happy to stick with what I have grown used to and can keep down comfortably, especially if I am going to a restaurant.

15th December having dinner tonight at The Cock & Rabbit at The Lee, haven't been there for some six years, Michael & Julie haven't seen us for several months and they were very surprised to see me neat and trim. So the band has been doing its job. Have eaten sensibly in the restaurant tonight and was very glad to get home, very tired as I had been with the horses all day. I haven't eaten any chocolate for 10 days.

18th December have been to the Luggershall Carol Service where I saw many of my old neighbours who I see two or three times a year as we live right out in the countryside and our nearest neighbour lives half a mile up the road. Again they were quite surprised to see how small I am compared with this time last year. Having seen people tonight that I haven't seen for a very long time they were surprised at the difference in me and I can't tell you how thrilled I am with myself let alone how thrilled I am that other people are recognizing how well I have done. Really looking forward to going skiing this year, we leave on 24th December.

19th December seen Dr Watt my GP today who was very pleased with my progress and asked me if I would recommend the procedure to anybody else if I was asked, I said I would because it has completely turned my life around.

20th December had a drink with my friend Sue who came on the Peru trip with me. We had a good laugh about how she was sick with altitude the whole time and how I was sick because of the state of the food. Had a very amusing evening and it was good to see her, she was very pleased that the nibbles she dished up I managed to eat and keep down. These consisted of Hummus and cheese & onion crisps as she knows all the time we were away I was longing for Hummus and cheese & onion crisps. Not particularly good for the diet and on the way home I confess I stopped and bought a bar of Galaxy chocolate in the garage – my Christmas present to me!

CHAPTER 5

One Year On

23rd December my last day at the stables for the Christmas period and Elizabeth, one of the women who comes to the stables has made my day, she said every time she sees me she thinks I am getting thinner and I think she is absolutely right. She thinks it is because Bumble is working me too hard (the lady whose stables I work at) but of course it is the band that is really the secret but that is my personal business and no-one else's. Did drink rather a lot of champagne as my favourite horse has been sold for a huge amount of money, he has to pass the vet now so we started celebrating Christmas very early and let's just say Merry Christmas!

24th December Thomas, his girlfriend, Steve and I are all off to Stanstead to fly out to Lyon for a week skiing. I have been into W.H. Smith at the airport, bought some fruit allsorts. Went for breakfast where the others ate a full English breakfast and I ate a piece of toast – good old band keeping me on the straight and narrow. Would love to have eaten a piece of bacon but know very well I wouldn't be able to digest it. Quick tip to anyone who loves bacon as much as I do you can buy bacon bits in a jar from Tesco and mix in with just about anything, they are easy to digest. They are also very easy to cook especially with mashed potato in the microwave.

25th December I have skied all day like a champion with my son, his girlfriend and my husband. We have skied from top to bottom all over Val D'esére, a little short of snow and we were last off the slopes. I am starving hungry, looking forward to the food tonight and hope I can keep it down. I had a bowl of soup up the mountain, also some mulled wine as it was minus 15 but I didn't need that excuse. Very different to last year on Christmas day, I sat at the top of the mountain in Obergurgl and drank hot chocolate all morning, miserable, fat, uncomfortable, hating myself, looking forward to arranging with Shaun Appleton to give me the operation I so needed to stop me binging, pigging out and thoroughly making a mess of myself weight wise. It felt so good today to ski all day not feel tired, have good balance, be able to go at a good speed and ski any run in front of me including a couple of mogul fields. We came back via Tigne so had a very good ski, wonderful, so much better than last year, I cannot tell you how much better than last year, what a difference the band has made to my lifestyle.

Our room is on the top floor of the chalet, four flights of stairs up so just as well I have no weight to carry as in ski boots up and down those stairs is a lot of hard work. But being fit and nimble as I am now I didn't find it difficult at all, last year it would have been a very different story. I would still be trying to climb the first flight!

30th December, Steve's 50th birthday, had my picture taken sitting on his knee with us both holding a glass of champagne, have to say didn't look quite as slim as I thought I did so will be having the band tightened when I return.

31st December home today and out tonight to celebrate New Year's Eve. Went to our friends at Rigoletto's and had a good evening. Happy New Year to 2006. We did eat at The Golf Club buffet, I struggled a bit but I know I still need the band tightening so on the 3rd January I shall make an appointment to see Mr Appleton to have it filled to 8ml.

3rd January 2006 back at my desk and oh! I am so sorry to be sat here. I had a wonderful Christmas, a fantastic New Year's Day with the horses and made an appointment to see Mr Appleton on 5th January to have the band tightened by ½ml. I can eat too much. Today I have eaten a piece of cod from the chip shop with lots of salt and vinegar, not good for me, must have the band tightened. I am a little nervous of having the other ½ml in but it is essential.

5th January is here I have come out of the Chiltern Hospital where Mr Appleton has given me a further ½ml, have to say I was absolutely petrified, talked 19 to the dozen but it was all unfounded because I didn't feel a thing. He was pleased with my progress, delighted to see me looking so fit and well and when I drank the glass of water after having the ½ml put in I walked round the car park while I sipped it and then for another 10 minutes to make sure it stayed down. Arrived home and had a cup of hot milk, a tablespoon of mashed potato with Bertolli spread. I feel very full and going to bed having an early night but feel very pleased it was a success having the band tightened today.

6th January, first day with the band at 8mls, feel great, for breakfast I had one yogurt bar and a glass of milk. For lunch I had two scrambled eggs and half a piece of toast and for supper I had the equivalent of three tablespoons of mashed potato with bacon bits and Bertolli spread on the top. Feel great and don't feel sick, haven't tried to eat anything solid, I did bring up a little of the toast but on the whole had a very good day and I think the band is probably tight enough although it doesn't seem massively tight.

7th January have eaten out for the first time this evening since having the band tightened, managed to eat a little fish and paté. The band is tight enough, the weight appears to be falling off me although I can drink plenty and can still eat reasonable amounts. I am on the mashed potato and softer foods have plenty of energy though and feel really good.

8th January Sunday evening, had a good day overall but tried to eat some Chinese special fried rice, home cooked no fat and the band has not liked that one bit, it stuck and made me feel as if I were going to choke so I will give that a miss in future. I mixed a few prawns with it along with soy sauce and finely chopped cabbage but have not been able to swallow this at all.

9th January managed to eat a Weetabix this morning and mashed potato with mince & gravy for lunch and half a cheese sandwich for my tea. I think the band is tight enough and the weight is coming off me, still full of energy, have been gardening this afternoon so we make progress. I am now in training for Everest Base Camp.

11th January ridden out this morning 3 lots have now completed a 12 mile hike up and around Muswell Hill. Feel good and looking forward to going to Everest. Starving hungry on my return as had no breakfast ate one Weetabix and a cup of hot water. Went shopping this afternoon delighted to buy a pair of jeans size 12 fit with plenty of room feeling very pleased with myself.

16th January I have taken my measurements and in total have lost 40 inches all over, measuring my bust, my waist, my widest part, the tops of my arms and my hips and thighs. I am very pleased with the total of 40 inches. The eating is spasmodic I really need to stick to soft foods. Fish is my main source of food along with mashed potato. I am riding regularly, feeling very fit and healthy, taking the vitamins every day, essential part of equipment and I need to eat more vegetables, not able to do that so far.

20th January last night we went out to dinner and I managed to eat a piece of cod and a couple of spoonfuls of tomato soup but eating out not a strong point as my eating has been cut down. Today I have driven to London to take Thomas back and had a very busy week, feeling tired, haven't been able to eat anything very much all day. I have bought myself some V8 vegetable juice, 100% vegetable juice and some fruit juice. I am suffering a bit with constipation and have been doing so for a good 7 days. Prune juice is also being taken and hopefully I will feel a bit better with it all tomorrow.

Monday 23rd January today is supposed to be the most miserable week of the year but for me it is probably one of the best weeks I have had for many years, the weight is steadily coming off, the eating has improved, for instance this morning I had a cup of Options low calorie hot chocolate at six o'clock and at nine o'clock a scrambled egg on half a slice of toast, feel good it has stayed down so I think I have now adjusted to the band being at 8ml. The vegetable and fruit juice I had over the week-end has also given me a boost so feeling good. Looking forward to riding out at the racing stables tomorrow. It is only approximately six weeks until I do the trek to Everest Base Camp. One slight problem I forgot to mention is my hair has started to fall out in handfuls so I am going to speak to the nutritionist today. Having spoken to the nutritionist she told me my diet must be very poor and I need to increase my vegetable and fruit intake plus start to take a zinc tablet per day along with my multi-vitamin. Have explained how difficult it is to swallow fruit and veg. Her answer in a very firm tone was to liquidise both! This I will do…..

24th January rode out on the gallops this morning at my new stables, rode two lots and it felt great. Managed to have a leg up onto both of them so feeling agile, fresh and fit. Couldn't have rode like that on the gallops a year ago. I wouldn't have been able to ride for a start off because I was way too heavy. It is great riding at speed again. I am having dinner at the Cock & Pheasant at Wing tonight. Had a Dover sole, starving hungry, really worked up an appetite and thoroughly enjoyed it. What is more it stayed down.

26th January a year has now passed and it seems a life time ago I experienced this life changing operation. To be active fit and well is the most wonderful feeling whereas before I had become fat, lazy and dull.

3rd February had a great day today. I have ridden out at the racing stables for the second time, had a wonderful time. Four people today have told me I look as if I have lost a lot of weight so I feel on top of the world. I have been eating approximately two tablespoons of liquidized vegetables each day. Vast improvement as I hadn't been eating any vegetables hardly at all, so my diet in general has improved. Also been out to dinner tonight with some friends managed to eat comfortably soup, half a chicken breast with a little mashed potato followed by an Irish coffee. I had two spritzers as well and it all stayed down, feel very full but not as if I am going to puke it all up so feel much better with the eating today. I have to say I haven't eaten anything much throughout the day, my hair appears to have stopped falling out and I look better in myself, I think I have now adjusted to having the band tightened to 8mls. It is a great relief since I have been on the zinc tablets my hair has stopped falling out. Feel good and look forward to next week making sure my progress continues. Also weighed myself on the scales in Boots today and I have lost a further 4lbs since my weigh in with Mr Appleton. Different scales I know but still very encouraging!

5th February had some old friends I hadn't seen for 20 years for lunch. They have all had trials and tribulations, one lost his son, the other one has a son dying of cancer but apart from that they were on good form and we had a lovely lunch. I ate a minimal amount and managed to keep it down so felt good including a small amount of vegetables, mashed swede, mashed carrot and a few peas along with a Yorkshire pudding, couldn't face the beef but managed to eat the rest of it. Everyone said how well I looked and how neat and fit – wonderful.

6th February very constipated again this morning, therefore the scales are showing I am heavier than on Friday. I need to drink a small glass of prune juice every day otherwise I am not able to go to the toilet properly. Having liquidized vegetables each day and I think that is helping me have more energy and not looking so black under the eyes. So, although I feel great there is still a little room for improvement in my diet. Prune juice is an absolute must. I am about to go off riding down at the racing stables to ride the first lot and the time now is 6.30 in the morning.

Have ridden out two lots this morning, had a great ride on Little Con, she has won four races & also on General Patten, he galloped like a trouper, fantastic feeling and pleased to say don't feel half as knackered as I did four weeks ago when I first started. There would have been no chance to ride top class racehorses a year or so ago. What a wonderful feeling to be riding on a racing plate (saddle) at top level again aged 53, neat, fit & trim.

7th February, dentist, have been going to Mr Brocklehurst for some 20 years and he was amazed at how much weight I have lost and how fit I look so have come away from there for the first time feeling a million dollars. The dentist is the one thing I have a tremendous fear of, it is the needle factor that really gets me. We all have fears of some kind and mine is of needles as I am sure Mr Appleton is aware.

8th February having read over the diary of the last month I have proved to myself if I am not starving hungry and only think I am that's when the food will not stay down. Lesson learned only eat when very hungry and not out of habit.

9th February have been to the physio-therapist today. Ford is the physio for the bob sleigh Olympic team and is a friend of Steve's. He has worked my hips and back for the last five years and does a wonderful job. He is absolutely stunned at how fit I am again and needless to say my hip has improved tremendously in the last year.

11th February and Steve is away for the weekend. I am out with girlfriends each day and Sunday lunch with George. Had a good weekend, managed to eat a little bit of lunch at The Mole & Chicken. I had oxtail with mashed potato and managed to spoof that I was eating quite well because I ate the mashed potato and the juice from the oxtail. So, Uncle George did not notice that I couldn't keep much down.

I have to confess as Steve is away this week-end I haven't eaten one vegetable, how bad is that?

13th February and my diet is still far from right, although full of energy I am eating all the wrong foods. I am eating crisps, yogurt bars, cream light cheese and stilton cheese. I think I have put on 3lbs. Steve has been away this week-end and I found it incredibly hard to stay on the straight and narrow with him away. I had stopped eating chocolate but instead I have been drinking chocolate milk drinks which are not as bad, as low in fat but high in sugar. It is a problem to get the balance right. I have been drinking the fruit juice but even now over a year later I am still struggling to improve my daily diet.

I am off to a point to point today with some friends and I am worried about having a proper lunch with them in case I can't keep the food down. I have to tread very carefully on that front, also I will need to try very hard today not to eat high sugar content foods.

Today has been freezing cold and I was only too glad to get home. I had a cup of soup when I got home, this I am pleased to say did stay down and by golly I really needed it. I was so cold I was shaking.

14th February Valentines Day, went for a 2 hour walk and hiked round Muswell Hill so walked 13 miles and six of those miles were up hill, feel wonderful. For Valentines night Steve took me to the Indian in Long Crendon, my favourite but unfortunately the food was a little cold. Managed to eat a bit, but not a great deal. Had my usual chicken korma, ate the sauce, no chicken and a little sag aloo, not a great deal but managed a poppadom and sauce and it all stayed down.

16th February another long walk ate my food on the hoof so to speak, walked for 13 miles again six of those miles were up hill and had a cheese sandwich in brown bread which stayed down. Drank near enough a litre of water and one bar of chocolate, all stayed down, feel wonderful but very tired and went to bed.

18th February had some V5 vegetable juice this morning also fruit juice as constipated, had prune juice and hopefully that will move something sometime soon. Even with all the exercise I have been doing the riding out and walking to get ready for Everest Base Camp still constipated. Slight problem.

19th February bowels worked, major improvement, feel much better.

20th February bowels worked again, rather like busses – all or nothing! I have been for a long walk, 13 miles and very tired at the end of it. Need to increase my calorie intake in some shape or form. I wouldn't say I am losing weight but I am not eating properly.

21st February Thomas' presentation for the Scales Prize at Stanmore did a wonderful presentation. Of course there were nibbles afterwards, didn't try any of those just in case any of them lodged, I wouldn't want any of the 30 doctors there to think I was ill. So just sipped a glass of mineral water and when I got back in the car I ate two yogurt bars, came home and had stewed vegetables Steve had cooked for me.

22nd February dentist day, D-Day, hate it had to take five valium as I had to have a nerve out of a tooth. Tried to eat a piece of fish afterwards and was violently sick. Lesson to be learned – do not try to eat when you are full of valium.

23rd February walked for 20 miles today and feel good. I have eaten a cheese sandwich, a packet of crisps and two yogurt bars and drank a litre and a half of water all on the hoof. It was a marvellous experience, thoroughly enjoyed it.

24th February Steve is away for the weekend so my diet I am sure will plummet. Have been to Tesco and bought a shepherd's pie and a fish pie. These will last me the whole weekend I am sure. Have been walking each day and enjoyed the fish pie so far. Had lunch with a friend at The Mole & Chicken on Sunday and had the same again, oxtail and mashed potato, easy because I can push it around the plate and because a lot of it is bone it looks as if I am eating well and nobody panics. Had a good day.

27th February. Not looking forward to tomorrow because I am going to see Mr Appleton to have 2mls taken out of the band. This afternoon saw my son and we went to Ask Pizza House. I managed to eat ¼ of a pizza before having to throw it up. Haven't eaten very well today, had a packet of cheese & onion crisps, how bad for me, no vegetables and no fruit juice. Constipated again, I will never learn I don't think.

3rd March. A very good exercise day as I have walked 12 miles, 5½ miles was up hill and walked at a very good pace, thoroughly enjoyed it lovely and sunny. Bad day food wise, having 2mls removed has been fatal. I have eaten a pork pie and a cheese & ham slice in thick pastry, this I micro-waved and the grease just ran out of it. What is worse I really enjoyed it. For my supper tonight I had a stir fry with pieces of bacon not so bad, also drunk 2 litres of water and ate half a bag of fruit allsorts. So the diet is still diabolical and I shall be damn glad when I have the 2mls back in so I can't eat vast amounts like I have today. I couldn't have managed a whole pork pie and I certainly couldn't have eaten a ham and cheese slice straight off, both of which I have done very comfortably today. I am hoping as soon as I start the Everest trip on Monday that the stuffing will stop because hopefully the band will tighten up due to the high altitude.

Chapter 6

Hiking to Everest Base Camp

4th March. Packing, have all my crisps, sweets and Go-Ahead yogurt bars also my antiseptic wipes! I have under15kg in weight looking forward to the journey and now ready for tomorrow.

5th March now at the airport and the time is 7.30 in the evening. Now ready for the long flight.

6th March arrived in Kathmandu after a long flight, it was good to have had the 2ml out of my band because it meant I could eat some of the food on the airplane this makes a change, however I am full up and haven't been able to gorge so that is a relief.

7th March had a terrible night, bad stomach and sure I have some sort of bug. Steve has been on the sight seeing tour by himself and met the rest of the group. At the moment I don't feel I could do the trek. Haven't been able to eat or drink anything all day, feel terrible, hope it's nothing to do with the band or the altitude but sure it isn't, absolutely sure it is a bug.

8th March feel very, very weak am going to try and go to Lukla with the rest of the group today. Boarded the little eight seater plane felt slightly queasy but have now arrived at Lukla. First view of the mountains and the Himalayas from the air is fantastic. Walked for three hours, feel very weak and managed to drink water only. I have needed the loo about seven times already today and it is not even evening yet, definitely not feeling well and I am very surprised I made the walk. It is wonderful to see the mountains around us and all the beautiful flowers but I am not feeling up to this. The camp site is at Phakding right by the river Dudh Kosi. This river is fast flowing, it is beautiful and Steve and I have washed our feet in it tonight. Steve also washed his shirt out and I have to say the cold water has made me feel much brighter. Experienced our first camping food and although I am sure it is of a very high standard haven't fancied it one bit but have drunk plenty of water, about 2 litres. I could do with some nourishment really but unable to take any.

9th March have walked for five hours today to Monjo, feel a little better but still pretty weak. Managed to eat a little porridge this morning, all I can say is hopefully the weight is coming off. The views are spectacular. Have eaten a tiny bit of food this evening but had terrible stomach ache. Had to walk round and round to try and ease it, I am hoping it is not the band - sure it isn't. The camp site tonight is horrible, smelly and disgusting. We are moving early tomorrow morning and hope I feel better.

10th March walked for four hours today arrived at Namche Bazaar it was very steep and felt terribly weak but managed it. We are staying in a little lodge tonight and have a day off tomorrow boy do I need it. Had our first view of Mount Everest today spectacular and looking forward to seeing it closer up. Have eaten one Mars bar, unable to eat the food, living on a couple of cups of hot chocolate today (so glad I brought some Options with me) and a little packet of Cheddar biscuits. I will be glad when this trip is over not enjoying it to date.

11th March - rest day. Feel a fair bit brighter, have been to the town of Namche Bazaar and we are at 3,440 metres high. I am very glad I had the band loosened as I think it has tightened up. I am able to eat things like soup and porridge today so feeling a lot better than I did. We had a heavy snowfall and have been cut off from the rest of our trip. We are going to have to go a different way. Everything looks stunning with the beautiful heavy snow. Hygiene is appalling and the rooms are freezing so I will look forward to moving on tomorrow.

Sunday 12th March walked for many hours in fact 7 hours today to Thyangboche and we have been to The Everest View Hotel where we saw Everest in all its glory with the sun shining on it. It was amazing, has made the last few miserable days worthwhile. Had several cups of hot chocolate today and feeling much better. Late afternoon we visited Sir Edmund Hilary's School also the hospital he funded, very pleased I have been here today. The statue of him looked alive, it was fantastic to see. Unfortunately the toilets are even more disgusting than all the others we have used and I shall be really glad to get back to civilisation. You could not call this trip a holiday you would call it an experience.

13th March this is my third and last night in a tent. We have been to the monastery at the village of Thyangboche, we saw the skiing monks who were very entertaining trying to ski on bits of half pipe in their long clothes all laughing and joking, slightly touristy perhaps but it was good entertainment value. Steve and I both made the decision that camping is not for us and I have got the right miseries. Steve's knees are killing him so we have decided to lodge it and I am sure life will become much better. I think the other people in our group are not too happy about this decision but to be quite honest I couldn't care less.

14th March we are now at Deboche and the camp site is in the most spectacular place. We have stunning peaks all the way around us - the climb to here was extremely steep. I am glad I have been able to eat a little porridge and some soup because the climb has been gruelling. We have seen the monastery of Khumbu and also climbed along the ridge viewing Amadablum, the most stunning peaks you can possibly imagine. It has been a very, very long walk. No more tents for us like I said. Everybody seems to have come to terms with this now. We are staying in a lodge consisting of four pieces of plywood with a toilet outside (a hole in the floor but with a sky blue porcelain bottom), the sheets are pure white on the mattresses. Not that we will be sleeping in them because we need to have our thick down sleeping bags to keep us warm. It has been extremely cold and even though we are in what they call a lodge it is very basic, in fact like I have just explained it is four pieces of plywood with a piece of wood for a bed and a thin stuffed mattress on the top. There is no light so we have to use a torch and the toilet like I say is a hole in the ground outside but at least it is not smelly, and we can both stand up to have a wash!

15th March. Today has been exceptionally long, we have walked for 9 hours. Steve and I led all the way, thank goodness we are fit otherwise it would have been sheer misery like everybody else is finding it. It has been steep with one part being very straight along a narrow path and exceptionally long. We are approximately 4,930 metres high and breath is hard to gain. The views are spectacular. If I hadn't had the bug I would have been feeling much better not quite as weak as I am. I found myself hallucinating on the last two hours and have drunk nearly 4 litres of water today, carrying it has been a killer but essential. The views of Nuptse, Lhotse, Chhukung Peaks and Injatse are all in view surrounding the valley. We walked around the ridge and it has been a tremendous hike. Everybody is now in lodges because the snow is too deep and snowing heavy, we have seen massive glaciers draped beneath the cliffs that sour up to 3,500 metres in the same dramatic valley. It has been amazing, glad I have made it, glad I stuck at it but it has been hard. I had to start using my inhalers as I am asthmatic.

16th March and by golly have we experienced the worst toilets ever not even buildings but tin sheds that stink. I have never seen so much human crap in all my life and I also learned the vegetables all look so healthy because they use human manure to fertilize them. It is what you could call organic, has put me off vegetables - never was very keen on them to start with but even less keen now. Still sticking to the soup and fortunately took some oxtail soup with me, the cheddar biscuits and Mars bars. Not very healthy I am afraid Mr Appleton but calories are a necessity and I am burning loads of calories!

17th March and arrived at Gorak Shep, the walk was hard and steep. We are now at 5,288 metres high, spectacular views of Everest and the new base camp. Gorak Shep is the original base camp. The snow is horrendous, very deep, but it is sunny, beautiful and can't believe I am here. I cannot believe I have made it, it has been absolutely killing. Anybody who says this trip is easy they are lying, this is hard. Even I have found it hard and I am fit, even though I say it myself. Anybody who reads this if they are going they want to make sure they are super fit otherwise you cannot enjoy it. The other five people in our group are miserable because they are not fit enough. It is an essential priority to exercise properly before you undertake the trip. We are surrounded by the most spectacular peaks here at Gorak Shep, we have Pumori at 7,145 metres, Lingtren at 6,697 metres and Nuptse at 7,745 metres and of course Everest at 8,848 metres. What a sight Everest is. It is still snowing, still bitterly cold -20 in the shade. I shall be very glad to be back in Kathmandu at The Radisson Hotel. Can't bear the toilets, I have come to Nepal to see Everest but all I can remember most of the time is how awful the toilets are. In fact they have been so awful they put a tent up at each stop especially for me otherwise I am vomiting all the time, so thank you to the guide who has taken mercy on me and erected a tent at every stop – thank you so very much.

18th March. We were up at half past five this morning it is freezing cold and we set out to trek up Kala Pattar Mountain, but I only made it a third of the way and my inhalers froze along with my hands. I have snow bite on both my little fingers and was unable to breathe at 5,320 metres so had to turn around at 5,320 metres. Very disappointed but I couldn't go on. Steve made it, the only one from our group, and has done extremely well. It absolutely shattered him. Turned around tonight and now on our journey back,walked for 6 hours today in total. A very long day and even though we are coming down it seemed a long, long way. My breathing still hasn't recovered from this morning, I have been on the hot chocolate and soups so feeling pretty weak, drunk lots of water and been trying to eat Mars bars just to keep the calorie count up. It has been a massive strain doing this and I have been hallucinating walking back. I arrived back at our accommodation at Pheriche two hours before Steve. The accommodation is a little better than normal although the toilets absolutely stink. When Steve arrived back he was totally exhausted and we haven't eaten the camp food tonight. We had in-house food, not a great deal better but it looked cleaner. Steve had tomato soup and chips I had mashed potato with grated cheese and felt much better for it. Sat by the burning fire (Yak dung) and I didn't think I would ever be quite so pleased to see so much animal crap in all my life, but the heater has made the place warm and that is a real bonus when you have nearly frozen to death up a mountain.

The Yaks are beautiful creatures and I love the sound of their bells except when they sit outside our little hovel of a night ringing them so we don't get any sleep, but we have been up at 6.30 each morning at the latest and been going to bed at about 8 o'clock every night. Tonight Steve was in bed by half past 6 and I don't think he is going to stir until tomorrow morning – very unusual for him.

19th March. We walked back for 9 hours to Deboche. This is where the climbers for Everest stay, a nice little camp site. We are in the lodge and our room is right above where the fire boiler is down below. Our room is warm, the first time our room has been warm since we started this never ending hard gruelling trip. We are delighted we can sleep with just two coats on not three, in two sleeping bags not three and also with only two pairs of long thermals on instead of three. It might sound unbelievable but we have on more clothes to go to bed throughout the whole trip than we have been putting on during the day. Haven't had a shower for five days, can't wait to have a shower and hopefully tomorrow will be that day.

The weather has been really good, very sunny during the day, cold in the shade but hot in the sun. We had our last view of Everest today a great shame but if nothing else I could always say I have seen Everest and Everest Base Camp and that has always been a dream. Without the band, without losing the weight, without getting super fit again I would never ever have experienced this. It has been magnificent just to see it and to have managed the trek. Yes two trekking days to go, but the main of it is over. We have met some interesting people, some very nice people, all nationalities, but it has been a long hard slog.

20th March have walked for 6 hours today and climbed up a very steep mountainside, on hands and knees. Even the sheep have a job to claw their way. Saw the school house in the clouds that Sir Edmund Hilary funded in Khunjung. We are now back down to 3,780 metres high feeling much better and looking forward to our last camp site tonight.

21st March - Phakding this is the very first camp site we stayed at but we are no longer camping we are in the lodge, some of which had no windows, some had tiny windows, some had Yaks with their heads virtually in the tiny windows, some had all sorts of rubble under the beds, others just big open spaces with dirt underneath the bed, talk about primitive, third world not for me, very sorry. I feel I have done my bit now and looking forward to some home comforts. The camp site we are at is OK - a party this evening gone pretty well, the guides, the cooks, the sherpas and the porters have all been exceptionally good. They all work so very hard and I can't believe people can work like they do for £2.00 a day - appalling. Anyway I can honestly say I have enjoyed seeing the sights, I wouldn't do it again but it has been a tremendous experience and one I wouldn't have missed. Not to be repeated, have been there, got the t-shirt.

Wednesday 22nd March we are now back at Lukla where we started from and have walked for 5 hours. Had my first shower for 6 days and wow it felt wonderful even though it was only a little trickle. Had to wear my backpacker sandals in the shower because it was really grimey, couldn't care less kept the shoes on. I had a cheese sandwich which tasted wonderful even though the bread was stale. Went for a walk in the town which is filthy but it was nice to be able to walk among a few shops who sold fake North Face goods. We catch the plane tomorrow back to Kathmandu and looking forward to it.

23rd March have flown back to Kathmandu today back to The Radisson Hotel. Oh! Five Star luxury. I will never ever moan about anything ever again having survived this trip. The trekking has been spectacular, the people so hospitable, the views magnificent, the toilets disgusting and the views of Everest out of this world. The two things I will always remember this trip for are:-

1) The toilets – never to be forgotten
and
2) The views of Everest and the Base Camp – absolutely magnificent.

Looking forward to going home, completed my shopping today consisting of North Face fake goods for Thomas my son. Steve and I enjoyed a proper meal in the hotel tonight. I had a cheese burger, excellent. Steve had a steak...... civilisation at last!

26th March. Home and looking forward to having the band tightened on Tuesday as I can eat pretty well.

28th March I have been to The Paddocks Hospital to have the band tightened and it made me feel funny as always. It was good to see Mr Appleton, told him how fit I feel and that I needed the band tightening but very glad he loosened it because it was obvious it tighten up at high altitude. The one thing I did forget to tell him was whilst in Kathmandu

I bought a North Face coat in an extra small size and did that make me feel good. I start riding the horses again in a week's time, once I get over the jet lag, and looking forward to that so 5th April here I come back at the racing stables.

29th March the band has 2mls back in so I have 8mls and I cannot eat, can only drink liquids. Not looking forward to going out on Friday night because I don't think I am going to be able to eat properly.

31st March the band has definitely stopped me eating, tried to eat Scampi Provencal and have been as sick as a dog. I haven't been able to keep anything down apart from liquids, did manage an Irish coffee and one white wine spritzer, not very good, no food – nothing solid so far to date. I know this is the run of the mill of things after having had it tightened for over a year but it doesn't become any easier when you have to keep excusing yourself from the dining table. I will persevere and if it hasn't loosened off a bit by the end of next week I will go back to have it slightly loosened hopefully that will not be necessary.

Sunday 2nd April the band must have slackened a little because I managed to eat a small stir fry, very well cooked, and it has stayed down so feeling better.

4th April went to London to see Thomas, bought three hot sausages on the way to the station and ate two of them very slowly but puked them straight up. I shared a bowl of soup with Tom but must have had a piece of sausage lodged because I couldn't drink it and brought that up as well. So lesson to be learned - chew things properly and give the sausages a miss.

Went to Starbucks, had a coffee and that stayed down. On the way home, not to be beaten by the sausages, ate the third remaining cold one I had bought very slowly and it stayed down.

5th April rode the horses this morning, wonderful experience and glad I felt so fit and light. This morning I had two tablespoons of Ready Brek before I went. This stayed down, first thing since yesterday and the sausage episode, also managed half a glass of cold milk. For lunch I haven't been able to keep anything down tried to eat half a cheese sandwich and brought that up. Kept hot chocolate down so I think I must still have a piece of sausage lodged. However feeling fit and very slim!

8th April, up bright & early to go to the racing stables. Have dropped two bra sizes now 38B this morning and it feels much more comfortable, I was 42B before. Feeling very pleased about this, it seems to have taken forever, just over a year, probably could have done it a couple of months ago but it feels right now.

11th April had a morning in my office and felt hungry all morning. Although I ate a cheese & beetroot sandwich I did bring it back up. I have eaten really well today, I had scrambled egg on toast for breakfast, a yogurt bar and a sandwich for lunch (although I couldn't keep down the sandwich), mid afternoon I had a packet of cheese & onion crisps – not very good - and this evening a finely chopped bacon salad I thoroughly enjoyed it so not too bad a day. Wondering if I might need to have the band tightened a little more, hopefully not. I feel very good in myself and now over the tiredness, jet lag and over exertion from the Everest Base Camp experience.

12th April feeling good, the band for me has cut down the amount I was eating. It has cut down the type of food I can eat as I am still unable to manage things like steak and lamb - basically red meat. I also have difficulty in digesting salad and vegetables that are not really well cooked. It doesn't stop me eating high calorie foods such as crisps, rich sauces, chocolate or anything that can be melted down or liquidized. So a little willpower is needed, but because the portion size and quantities have been vastly cut a little bit of what you fancy does you good like cheese & onion crisps and the odd bar of chocolate!

14th April bought a bike today my hip is too bad to ride the race horses so I have changed stables. I thought by losing all the weight and getting really fit the problem would go away but it hasn't. I feel very disappointed about that, I want to retain my level of fitness, whilst being at the racing stables and having completed the Everest Base Camp Trek, so have bought a pedal bike. I understand they are supposed to be very good for exercise and keeping you fit so I am going out on it tomorrow as we are off to London today. Have eaten out this evening with friends, ate a bowl of pea soup. I also had a piece of baked cod with olives, very nice, managed to keep it all down but that is all I have eaten today. So managed to cut back, but as I stood on the scales this morning I looked as if I had put on 2lbs. I was horrified but it is because my diet has been so poor, living on cheese & onion crisps and chocolate and Easter hasn't helped but no excuse.

15th April been for a fifteen mile bike ride today and nearly killed myself but my stomach has gone back in line to where it was. Exercise is so important to me I don't want to look unfit and have a big belly again, very conscious of this. Out for Sunday dinner this evening and managed to eat half a chicken breast, one roast potato and a small Yorkshire pudding. I also had an Irish coffee and a spritzer. Have not eaten very much today mainly because I was too knackered, when I came back from the bike ride. I really miss the race horses but know exercise is the most essential thing to keep myself fit, in shape and the weight off. Even though I have the band to stop me gorging it doesn't stop me eating high calorie food unfortunately, just stops me eating huge volumes of anything.

20th April have decided I can still eat too much. Although I am having a job to digest bread I am able to eat a whole decent sized jacket potato with cheese & butter also several yogurt bars to fill me up. A bit disappointed I am managing to consume quite so much in one sitting. So, I think I will have to go back and have my band tightened to 8½ ml.

21st April, feel a little depressed today can really eat - managed two rounds of sandwiches today. They were thick with Stilton cheese and light crisps inside the sandwich. I can visibly see the fat tyre appearing underneath my bust and the scales are showing I have put on 4lbs. Horrified – have tried to speak with Mr Appleton today but unfortunately he is completely busy for the next week. I won't be able to see him for 9 days. Goodness knows how big and fat I will be by then but certainly could have done without going for that long without having it tightened. I should have tried to see him today really but I was hoping I could control my appetite, but I can't. I don't know if the band has stretched or not but feeling very despondent at the moment. It's not helping that my hip is hurting and unable to ride like I could, so all in all not a good day today. I have made an appointment to have the band tightened on the 2nd May at 6.00pm.

23rd April feel depressed. Rode the horses today and felt fat & bulky on them. Feel I am slipping back into my old ways, bought a load of junk, two packets of cheese & onion crisps, a packed of Fruit Allsorts and two bars of Milky Way. I ate them all very comfortably and have also eaten four sausages (which I did bring back up). This evening I managed a bowl of stilton & broccoli soup (horrible - but still ate it), one slice of bread with thick butter, half a lamb stew with two dumplings and sweet mashed potato, an Irish coffee and one white wine spritzer. I have also eaten four yogurt bars containing 350 calories in total. Definitely feel depressed, don't know what to do about it, can't wait to see Mr Appleton to sort the band out and just hoping nothing has gone wrong like the liquid has come out for instance as I can eat so well. Yesterday I confess I ate a Burger King Extra Large - consisted of two beefburgers, tomato, mayonnaise and lettuce in a bun. Also ate half a dozen chips, these are something I haven't had for a very long time, as I no longer enjoy them. The port appears to be protruding more and seems to be higher up as if it has moved on my left side, so again I will be glad when Mr Appleton has seen this.

I can't remember the last time I felt so fed up, probably a long time ago before I had the band done. I did think my hip would be 100% ok once I lost the weight and fit, but it really has curtailed my riding and physical work so that isn't helping my mental state. I will probably have to see Dr Watt to have the hip looked at professionally. Have been putting this moment off because really don't want to be officially told what is wrong with it.

A lot of the problems could be down to my HRT and water tablets being out of sync after having completed the Everest trip with the time difference still affecting my body. The depression could also be down to this.

24th April - another testing day for the band. Because I feel out of control with my eating I feel as if I am testing the band to its full limit the whole time to see what I can force down my throat. I had an egg & bacon banjo sandwich consisting of three slices of bacon, two egg yokes and two slices of bread, most of this I kept down. For lunch I had a 4" long piece of French stick cut in half with low fat cheese and half a tomato, again most of which I kept down. For my tea this evening I ate a 6" length of French stick cut in half with 2oz of very thin Tesco finest ham and mustard I have more or less kept this down as well.

Having typed this it doesn't sound quite as bad as it has felt, but I feel as if I have been eating all day. It is probably because I had to eat the crusty bread very slowly in order to digest it, but I feel as if I am pigging out all the time. I feel very out of control and what concerns me is I only have one more mil for the band to be at its tightest. So feeling very unsettled and will be relieved when I have seen Mr Appleton to discuss it next Tuesday. What is worrying me more mentally is I feel I am pigging out and not exercising. I know I have a bad hip but I could have gone out on the bike this evening but didn't and I feel very disappointed with myself. I still feel as if I am having a mood swing about the eating being out of control.

The confession for the day is that I have eaten a cream cake today. I stuffed it and I normally hate cream cakes, they are something I never eat but today I just ate the biggest cream cake you ever did see, really, really bad! Very disappointed with myself and didn't even look like puking.

26th April. Pleased to say my hair has stopped falling out, the weight is piling back on, rode my bike yesterday afternoon and felt better for doing so. The hip is still bad, but eating wise yesterday I had porridge for breakfast, mashed potato with sweet corn and prune juice at lunchtime, for my evening meal I had sweet corn, mashed potato, cheese sauce and a piece of cod. I feel a little better mentally this evening.

27th April went riding this morning, a beautiful day, feel better in myself also out on the bike. Food wise still eating sweets but have eaten a better balanced diet. Very conscious that I am going to Ireland next week and do not want to be stuffing myself so glad I am having the band tightened. The mood swings appear to have stopped. Have completed a 25 mile bike ride this evening felt great at the end of it and eaten 2 sausages, a jacket potato with 2oz of grated cheese, and an ounce of chopped ham over a period of 3 hours. I feel miles better mentally for having made the effort to do the exercise. Becoming a couch potato does not stimulate the mind like hard exercise. Believe me I know!

28th April, had lunch with Tom in London today and the band must be working because I had a fish risotto for lunch. This stuck and wouldn't go down. I have eaten lots of sweets again and although I feel really negative from an eating point of view I feel very positive about having the band tightened. I know the pound I have put on, which I think this morning felt like six, will soon come off. I am hoping when it is tightened by ½ml it will be tight enough and not too tight because I am sure my HRT has something to do with the eating binge along with the time changes, the vomiting and the bug I had whilst in Nepal. I had a single portion of Marks & Spencer's pasta carbonnara for my tea as I am on my own this evening. This stayed down - a bad thing - but I thoroughly enjoyed it and made the most of being able to eat something I will not be able to eat when the band has been tightened. Still very constipated so continuing to drink the prune juice. My bust is very tender another sign of HRT being out of synch with the rest of my body.

29th April woke up with my bust extremely swollen and tender this morning, walked the dogs and felt really uncomfortable. I am also constipated, have drunk another glass of prune juice so hopefully some action later today. Rode the bike for only six miles today but thoroughly enjoyed it, have not ridden the horses because my hip is painful. Went out to dinner this evening, ate delicious homemade mushroom soup to start followed by a chicken breast in a pastry case with white wine sauce. Had two white wine spritzers and an Irish coffee so not a particularly healthy meal but thoroughly enjoyed it and it stayed down. I felt uncomfortably full afterwards and considering I had only eaten a yogurt for breakfast this morning I feel my eating is back under control. So, not sure whether the HRT is kicking back in, my body doesn't feel as if it is. My stomach does not seem so hungry and my mental state is much better. Hopefully I am on the road to recovery and the weight I have put on will start to disappear. My jeans feel tight and I have a roll of fat underneath my bust this I didn't have a couple of weeks ago, or even ten days ago. Disappointed with that but the power of positive thinking here - keep riding the bike and keep moving about – do not sit watching the television. Major lessons, what's more I know better than to sit watching the television.

One thing that cheered me up today, I looked at the photographs taken before the operation, (15 months ago) and the photographs taken back in February this year, the difference is incredible. That bucked me up and made me realise how well I have done. This kicked me into not feeling despondent about having put on a little bit of weight. Although six pounds is quite a lot of weight, it is only a little bit compared with what I have lost in total. Facially the double chins have gone, my legs do not rub together any longer when I walk, and my arms and tops of my legs have tightened up due to the exercise I have been doing. I only have one roll of fat on my back instead of three. My stomach looks considerably flat rather than protruding like it did 15 months ago. So roll on Tuesday looking forward to having the band tightened, and for the first time ever not dreading it because I know it is a tremendous help. I know I need it this time. I have been unable to sleep properly because it has been weighing on my mind so much that I have put on some weight and my biggest fear is of the whole lot piling back on. I think the only reason I am looking forward to having the band tightened is the fear of getting big and bulky again. Having put on these few pounds I don't feel so agile or nimble and it is a major, major fear with me that I will not be as active as I like to be. I also want to be able to wear skimpy tops and shorts in the summer again instead of big long baggy shorts – more incentive to improve the diet and not eat huge amounts. Of course, that is why I have the band, to stop me eating huge amounts. Unfortunately it cannot stop me eating sweets, rich sauces and drinking Irish coffee – only I can do that.

1st May my bust no longer feels tender, my eating seems to have reverted back to being under control, not sure that I really need the band tightened now but am going to see Mr Appleton tomorrow. Yesterday I had one sandwich to eat, about 2oz of humous, one scrambled egg on toast and three cups of Options low calorie hot chocolate so feel much better in myself. Didn't do any exercise yesterday because my bike had a puncture and the horses were going to an endurance race, so a day at home and had a good rest. I have ridden three horses this morning.

2nd May arrived back from The Paddocks Hospital after a good chat with Mr Appleton. The band has not been tightened. I knew deep down that it would not happen because it only has one mil to go, I have only had it in for a year and a half and overall I have made good progress. I have learned how to abuse the band that really is the truth of the matter. By standing up I can eat more, I eat all the wrong foods, sweets, sweets and more sweets and also cheese & onion crisps, although I have more or less managed to knock them on the head. I have also learned that if I eat slowly I can still eat fair size meals, like a whole jacket potato with sweet corn as I have today. But having had a good talking to I feel a little more in control and I know for this to succeed 100% I have to change my eating habits - I do know that! I had put on ¾ of a kilo (in other words 1½ lbs), I shall see how I go this next month and if I put on any more weight I will have to have another ½ml put in. Hopefully I won't have to and will have myself back in control. I feel bitterly disappointed with myself but I am very glad I have spoken to him about it and that I have been 100% honest - I have given myself a slap on the wrist. I also need to do more exercise than I am doing now that I am not race riding, so I shall have to find an alternative. Besides the biking and the riding I need one more thing so I think I will probably have to go to aerobics on a Tuesday evening.

I do think the support group will be a help not only to me but to everyone as it gives you someone else to talk to about the band. My husband, Steve, I am sure must be fed up with me talking about dieting and food all the time, the same as I become fed up with him talking about rugby. I know Mr Appleton suggested I see Jane the dietician again as she might be able to help me, but I really don't feel I need to see her because she is only going to tell me things I already know. That is probably why I don't want to see her because

I don't listen to what she tells me. Not good - I know I am doing wrong. So, maybe the support group might be helpful to me I will wait and see.

3rd May got up feeling much more positive this morning, up at six o'clock out on my bike by 6.30 and have done my 11¾ mile cycle ride feeling much better for it. It has cleared my mind and I returned to eat a bowl of porridge. I had a drink of water before I went this morning and a drink of water on the way. This I took with me. All the vitamins are in place, all my tablets are in place, and hopefully my eating will improve no end, although I do feel I have stretched the band a bit because I can eat crusty bread. I have been trying unsuccessfully now for 18 months to alter my eating habits and today is the day I am going to try to eat vegetables and salad. If they stick badly I know the band is still well and truly in place. I decided to fill in a food chart on a regular basis again so as to have myself on the straight and narrow. I noticed my stomach gurgles a lot whether this is because the food is passing through quicker I am not too sure. I need to remember to have a break in between eating, just finished my porridge so need to have a 15 minute break before I try some fruit to see if I am full up.

For lunch I ate chicken breast and my first piece of fruit probably since I had the operation. I had a piece of pineapple, a grape and I am very pleased to say they lodged (so the band is well and truly in place) even if it has stretched a little. I did have to bring the grape back up, probably will give grapes a miss in future or need to chew them twice as much. Sometimes I just never learn. I have eaten my first proper salad tonight since I had the band fitted. It consisted of breast of chicken, lettuce, radish, sweet corn and tomato, ate it very slowly, it took me an hour and fifteen minutes to eat but I have to admit it has filled me up. I also managed a slice of melon for afters so for today, although it is only 7.30 in the evening I have had a very healthy eating day – long may it last. The only things I brought up today, was a grape which stuck and I couldn't digest it.

3.00am in the morning on 4th May, leaving for County Cork in Ireland to see my niece. I had a tablespoon of porridge and half a glass of water. We had a good flight, arrived in Ireland, picked up the hire car and drove down to where we are staying. The countryside is so pretty and for lunch I had half a minute steak sandwich. This took me half an hour to eat and a cup of hot chocolate. For dinner I ate a bowl of mushroom & potato soup and a salad so I feel I have eaten very healthily today, but I do confess I had an Irish coffee and two white wine spritzers not so healthy. Overall I feel proud of myself, walked a round trip of 6 miles today but haven't been to the loo so still very constipated. All in all I have had a good day, in control, feel much better in myself.

5th May one slice of bacon with no fat for breakfast with half a slice of bread and two healthy Options hot chocolates (the equivalent to a mug). Went for a mile and a half walk and pleased to say my bowels have worked 100% so I feel much, much better as it is the first time I have been to the loo properly since I came back from the Everest trip. I would imagine I have now lost the 1½lbs I had put on just from that experience alone. Went to see the Blarney Stone today – did not kiss it!

6th May so far so good, no Go-ahead bars, slight panic as ate 2 chipolatas for breakfast with a slice of toast, one glass of water and a cup of Options hot chocolate. Feel guilty about the chipolatas as they have stayed down. Finding it difficult, to mentally adjust to not throwing up every time

I eat something solid. I had to chew, hence constant worry of putting on weight. Now realise I have been eating only very soft foods most of the time e.g. mashed potato, sweet corn, porridge, scrambled egg, thick soup, pizza, Go-ahead bars, crisps, low fat cheese, bread with thick Bertolli spread. Have realised how bad my diet has been as now keeping written diary of everything I put in my mouth like I did at the start after having the band fitted. The penny has suddenly dropped or reality has kicked in good and proper to how there is no green to be seen! What a difference eating the salad first has made – feel full afterwards and not craving sweet things. This has been the fourth day without a sugar fix, except for an Irish coffee and three spritzers, but no chocolate or sugar lumps – vast improvement. I am no longer constipated, even though been sat driving the car all day. Youghal, Killarney, Bantry, Skibereen back to Youghal. I made the decision not to drink any more Irish coffees, one reason to feel proud of myself. Today I resisted a huge fluffy meringue – it would have slipped down through the band a treat – Mr Appleton's words still ringing in my ears 'I can't help you any more than I have' a harsh reality. His manner and his ability to handle fat people's mental state have much improved since our early meetings.

7th May – spoke too soon yesterday, chronic indigestion at 3.00am during the night. Vomited violently, all salad and the ½ sandwich I ate for lunch. I don't think I will ever be able to cope with bread on a regular basis – not a bad thing as full of carbohydrates and read in a magazine for my shape ie: carry most weight around my middle – carbohydrates are the worst food for me – another reason for not eating Go-ahead bars. One consolation it has reassured me the band is well in place – relief! Feel a bit weak as if I need a sugar fix – for this had 2 mugs of Options hot chocolate. Will make sure I always carry a couple of sachets from now on to stop the cravings, only 40 calories in each sachet.

Looking forward to going on my bike tomorrow, and cycling my one and a half hour ride (11¾ miles) lovely when sunny not so lovely when raining. While sat in Cork airport dictating this diary three women walked past me each weighing a minimum of 16 stone, walked is the wrong word, waddled would be more accurate. I was the same 17 months ago, major incentive to keep riding the horses and the bike. Unable to bear the thought of putting on an ounce let alone the 2½ stone again. Intend to be the smartest mum at Thomas' graduation, stay off the crisps, Go-ahead bars, chocolate & Fruit Allsorts.

8th May out on the bike at 6.30am, 11¾ miles – compromise between running and riding horses on the gallops – poor substitute but beggars can't be choosers. Legs are working as if I'm running, wind in my face as if I'm on the gallops and my mind relaxed as if doing both the other activities so major plus and thumbs up for the bike.

As Thomas predicted my hip doesn't hurt, strange thought it would. Wish I liked swimming but I don't – unable to bear my head in the water – can swim but would never ever be able to motivate myself to be up bright and early for a swim especially if it was raining outside even though going to get wet – no not for me! Important to have sport activity you enjoy and not one only because it is good for you e.g. the gym – fine for once a fortnight if need be but hate not being in the fresh air.

Sugar Mountain

9th May been to Tesco today bought 2¾ stone in bags of sugar and heaped them in the corner of my bedroom so I can see how much weight I have lost – constant reminder when I wake up and every time I walk into the room. Felt as if I needed a crane to lift it out of the car boot and I had been walking around with that lot! I will add to it as the weight comes off. Intend to see Mr Appleton once every 2 months for the following year, money well spent, also can be weighed at The Paddocks on the same scales. No mood swings to date without the sugar fixes – thought there would be – mind over matter. When finished with the sugar will donate it to charity, out of date stamp is 2 years! Hope I won't need the constant reminder by then. If I had carried on putting on 1½lb per month the 2¾ stone lost would be back on by the end of the year – horrifying and frightening thought. When I see mothers feeding their kids sweets I feel like shaking them and saying don't.

12th May a week and a half now past since our little chat and have kept to the straight and narrow – miracle. Water retention seems to have passed.

13th May seen Thomas today – totally stressed – finals nearly over. He is so thin & pale, not sure who will be the most relieved when he has finished him or me. Could have killed for a bag of Fruit Allsorts after leaving him today but didn't as thought of all the bags of sugar heaped in the bedroom – major deterrent.

17th May only 2 weeks till Thomas' results then we leave for 4 days in Singapore (had my 50th birthday there in Raffles Hotel and promised him I would take him when he qualified). That promise seems such a long time ago - 3½ years! Then back to Dubai for 5 days. Looking forward to wearing swim shorts and a bikini top. Have them laid on top of the bags of sugar so I can see how awful the bulges look around them! Serious incentive, don't know why I didn't do this before.

20th May enjoyed the 3 horses this morning, rode solid for 4½ hours in total. Starving when I got home, as rode bike to and back from the stables, killing as up hill nearly all the way, had mince and vegetables for lunch. Still behaving myself – I'm impressed even if I say so myself, especially as not very good at doing as I am told on anything let alone my eating habits.

25th May vomited today, ate ham sandwich for lunch too fast, very hungry after riding and bolted it down, didn't chew properly. I now always sit down to eat so nothing will slip through the band if not chewed properly (pictured Mr Appleton's face when I told him I had stood up in the noodle bar to eat fried rice - mortified) to let it go down easier!

30th May leave for Singapore in 4 days, fit and 44 inches smaller than 18 months ago, also lost 2¾lbs - have added another bag of sugar to heap. Constipated again even though I have been eating one salad every day and drinking a glass of 100% fruit juice, still not enough but much better than before.

2nd June today I have been told my son is a Doctor, I must be the proudest mum on this earth, what a wonderful day – can't believe it – he has been out celebrating and has phoned about a dozen times. I have bought congratulations balloons and written to Dr Thomas love from the proudest mum all over his bedroom mirror and decorated the house, the driveway and the car ready for collecting him tomorrow.

Had very little to eat today but four glasses of champagne. I think today I can be forgiven.

3rd June collected Tom from the station, he nearly died when he saw the car was covered in decorations and balloons especially as the taxi drivers all started singing congratulations when he walked towards the car. Being a shy person this was almost too much for him. Went out to dinner to the Mole & Chicken at Easington, fabulous food, had my usual soup and chicken en croute, ate it very slowly and kept it down.

4th June - off to Dubai and Singapore today. The weather here is rainy but it doesn't matter as off for a nice long flight with my son, quality time for 10 days. The flights were a little disappointing but we had quite a bit of champagne to celebrate and it has been a wonderful day having Thomas to myself for the first time for a long time. Ate quite well on the plane, stuck to what I know I can swallow, chicken. I have completely given up eating bread as it really doesn't like me. Arrived in Singapore and to our room in Raffles, Thomas was thrilled and it brought back happy memories for me of my 50th birthday. We had a beautiful meal served in our suite with a welcome cake and fresh fruit which is far more to Thomas' taste than cake and I didn't eat either so I felt quite proud of myself. More champagne, and an early night.

6th June walked all over Singapore - good from the exercise point of view as I have been sat on my backside for a couple of days. Noticed how stodgy and full I feel and how constipated I am I need the exercise that I have become so used to.

7th June walked around Singapore again, had a massage on my neck and shoulders because my right arm is still a little stiff from where the horse pulled it last year. It is much cheaper here than it is in England for a massage, only £5 for a back and shoulder massage. Feel much better, have walked a good 15 miles today in flip-flops I may add but because my legs are fit they did not ache at all and neither did my feet. Thomas of course did this very easily and comfortably. He is a fitness fanatic. It just proves how much exercise helps because he used to be quite tubby when his father first died, but once he started the exercise programme and sorted out his eating he became very slim. He makes sure I do not slouch along but I walk out when I am walking around the town with him.

9th June on to Dubai, fabulous trip and a little lazier time I expect here although we are bound to go around the shopping malls for a bit of exercise, and plenty of swimming as the pool is fabulous. In the next room to us is Charlotte Church and her boyfriend, the rugby player Gavin somebody or other, seem very pleasant.

10th June healthy breakfast this morning, stewed fruit for me and a glass of orange juice as I am dreadfully constipated, obviously not been having anything like the exercise I have been. Had a good walk around the shopping malls today as well as a really good swim but not my normal amount of exercise when I ride the horses.

12th June ate in Gordon Ramsey's restaurant tonight and managed to keep everything down. On the whole trip only had two days of puking my food because I have been very careful what I have eaten so as not to alarm Dr Tom with how sick I can be at times. Also been to the racing yard in Dubai of Sheikh Mohammed this was fantastic, had a lovely couple of hours there, saw the horses swimming for exercise. Looks like swimming maybe a must, although I have been doing so the whole holiday I am not over keen I must admit, but it works muscles I do not normally work, it is not weight bearing so my hips feel really good, plus it is warm so my hip is not playing me up at all – good news.

14th June now home and very pleased to say I have not put on any weight, even though I ate reasonably well while away. Thoroughly enjoyed the trip it was quality time, feel relaxed and glad of spending the time with Thomas as I realise now he is into the real world and will probably not come home so much. This saddens me and I hope it doesn't set me off binging but at least I know I cannot eat huge quantities of food any longer.

It has been wonderful to wear a bikini again on holiday and swim in the pool not feeling like a beached whale, it has been great to walk around the pool without feeling as if all my flab and fat is hanging over the sides and my legs rubbing together. Thank goodness that no longer happens and thank you band. It has been wonderful to wear really nice clothes to dinner of an evening, little strappy tops and elegant shoes again. My passion for nice shoes has been enhanced whilst in Singapore as I managed to buy four pairs of Giovanna for £10.00 a pair!

20th June all off to Royal Ascot today, Steve, Tom, Maurice (Tom's girlfriend) and myself to meet a party of 14 of Roy who is celebrating his 80th birthday. We were fortunate enough to be invited to his box on the new Ascot complex overlooking the finishing line. We all went feeling a million dollars, me included in a little silk outfit and feeling very slender and smart. My son couldn't get over how different I looked from two years ago. He was looking at a picture before we left of me with him and well words fail me because the transformation is incredible – no longer a blob. We had a great day, I hardly ate anything because even though the food was excellent I felt the first quail's egg that I ate lodge and needed to bring that up so didn't tempt fate any more. Some days I can eat some days I can't – not a bad thing.

Race Ride

25th June, ridden out Thursday, Friday & Saturday and today the 25th I am off to Hereford to ride in a race. It is a long time since I have competed in anything and now it is over I am very pleased to say I won by 20 minutes. It was an endurance race of 20 miles and I rode a little Arab horse it won easily by 20 minutes. I would never have been able to do this, two years ago, it felt great to be sat among the 25 year olds and beating them. My competitive spirit has returned.

27th June - Oh no dentist day! An hour and a half treatment and very concerned having to take so much Valium before I go always makes me hungry. Having had the treatment tried to eat a sandwich and vomited. I never learn, I just never learn, bread does not like me I should not eat it. I can manage pitta bread but not bread, but today because of the Valium I am feeling starving hungry and the stress of going to the dentist straight on the food and of course it has lodged and I have been sick.

30th June, out to lunch with Wendy one of my best friends, we went to the Mole & Chicken my favourite eating house. We had a leisurely lunch where I ate a few prawns and a chicken breast on a skewer along with some sparkling mineral water - very good. I am now into eating healthily on the whole, although it does go in fits and starts but still room for improvement with the vegetables and anything green.

CHAPTER 7

My Own Horse Once More

Sunday 2nd July pleased to say I have ridden four horses this morning and thoroughly enjoyed it. Also had some good news I am about to be given a horse by Pepe who own La Traverna restaurant in Windsor, haven't seen them for years, they gave an unexpected call to see if I would like Tremezzo. Pepe learned I am back to my old self, riding, and he thought it would be a nice gift. How generous is that? This horse cost 32,000 guineas as a yearling, he is now eight years old, has won approximately nine races. Looking forward to him arriving and it all helps with the keep fit programme.

4th July slightly stressed today, I had problems with a delivery for Thomas' flat – straight on the cheese & onion crisps – really bad habit of mine, but haven't had any for a long time. I ate one packet today and an ice-cream mars bar, very bad. Stress always does it, cannot stop that, something I must change in my mind.

5th July, very pleasant meeting with a guy called Neil Richardson had a leisurely lunch with him but he was after my business. It makes such a nice change for someone wanting my business instead of me having to sell my business. Ate a salad and mackerel fillet followed by lemon sorbet - keep looking at the heap of sugar – real incentive. Things are improving long may it last.

6th July haircut day and Francine my hairdresser has lost 3 stones since Christmas she is looking fantastic, she also thinks I look fantastic but of course she does not know about the band. Feel a bit of a fraud as she has lost 3 stones in seven months and it has taken me nearly 18 months to lose the same amount with the aid of the band.

7th July saw Sandra today and she is off to ventures new as her father sold his restaurant. She looks magnificent, six stones lighter since having the band fitted and feeling wonderful. She is exceptionally happy and what a great party we had with them tonight. Sad to see my old friends go from the restaurant but time moves on, also means I won't be able to pinch handfuls of chocolates any more when visiting the restaurant!

8th July Newmarket races and hopefully Emma who I help will win today. Her father is also riding he is 56 so another veteran riding in endurance racing. Jenny, Emma's mum, and I have taken the horses up, plenty of exercise, a two mile walk from the stables to the start. I have made this trip 7 times today so plenty of exercise in store for the week-end. Had a BBQ tonight – cooked salmon fillet, jacket potato and sweetcorn – very healthy.

9th July we started at half past four this morning, it has been an exceptionally long day, sweltering hot but the good news is Herbie finished sixth and rode fantastically, Emma's horse sadly went lame. Feel very tired, not home till midnight and driving back from Newmarket seemed never ending. Did not pig out, had a good day eating wise, have eaten one chicken breast on a skewer this I barbecued before I left Newmarket and throughout the day I ate a small tin of sweetcorn a yogurt for breakfast and lunch. Sleeping in a tent was horrendous but not too bad on the food front. The tent was really uncomfortable and there was only me in it. It was not so long ago that I would not have fitted in the tent let alone slept in it.

12th July and Tremezzo has arrived. Wow he is beautiful, can't believe my luck, looking forward to riding him up the gallops. Jill delivered him for me, she had not seen me for nearly 30 years, she said I didn't look hardly any different except heavier! Good job she didn't see me 18 months ago.

14th July, my old school friend Dawn has arrived and slightly horrified to learn I am going off race riding on Sunday but she said she didn't mind and was very pleased to see me looking so fit and healthy.

15th July we went out to dinner and also went swimming today great to not feel self conscious in the changing rooms or walking to the pool – wonderful for the self esteem.

16th July, off to Ludlow leaving home at 4.30am for the 25 mile endurance race. Came 2nd a bit disappointed but not sufficient to set me off binging. I ate a tuna salad and two yogurts plus two Lucozade drinks. They are not good as fizzy and the band appears to find the gas difficult to deal with.

17th July very stressful, extremely tired, Thomas starts work and he is a bundle of nerves. His flat also comes up for re-let and because he has started work a week earlier than he thought he was going to, I am now left in charge of setting up the flat and furnishing it ready for the new tenants to move in. The deliveries have been stressful so needless to say I have been eating junk today, packet of Fruit Allsorts, a packet of crisps, had yogurt and melon also prawns but could have done without eating the sweets. I have found it very stressful driving through central London it is enough to make anybody stressed, but the real stress is the delivery guy's who do not want to work or carry anything up the stairs as the lifts are not working. We are on the ninth floor so I do have a bit of sympathy for them. The exercise has been good for me as I had to unload the car, 6 trips in total!

18th July stayed overnight at the flat, beautiful view of Victoria Docks and the Millennium Dome. We are next door to the Excel Centre so the Motor Show is on and the security is high. The weather is fantastic and if it weren't for the planes from City airport going over every 15 minutes I would think I was in heaven. I have to be home by 6.30pm because I am due at the Shelburne Hospital for the obesity clinic meeting. Had to cancel this meeting as I still have one delivery that has not arrived at 3.00pm, very disappointed I was not able to go. I hope there will be another one as apart from Sandra I haven't met anyone else who has a band fitted.

19th July busy in my office today as been missing for best part of the week, complete chaos. Very hot so drinking plenty of water, had one Weetabix for breakfast, jacket potato for lunch with sweetcorn, cup of low calorie soup for supper with toasted pitta bread and a yogurt. Great news at the end of the day the flat has been let so Thomas is happy and I am happy, no longer stressed – good day.

22nd July prune juice is definitely a must to keep in the house, so constipated but think I have lost another two pounds. I will check again in 2 weeks as I would like to add another bag of sugar to the heap.

26th July my mother-in-law is coming to stay and everything is spic and span. She arrived and said how well and fit I look so that made me feel good. Went out to dinner at The Lion in Waddesdon, I ate very carefully to make sure I was not sick and had to excuse myself from the table, I had soup to start, followed by fishcake and a cappuccino. A very pleasant evening, if I look as good as my mother-in-law when I am 70 I shall be delighted.

27th July had my haircut by Francine, who has been dieting herself and has lost 4 stone, without the aid of a band but she still has another 5 stone to go. She was a very big lady but has worked very hard at it and hasn't cheated like myself, although I don't really believe I cheated just invested in my health and well being. Although I admire those, who manage without any added assistance. Francine looks extremely well and said she can't get over how much weight I have lost, but since she has known me I have really only lost a little less than her. It seems more because I am not very tall at 4'11". Sweets are still a problem but I am trying to eat healthier, really, really trying. Still taking the vitamins every day and I feel good.

28th July a very good afternoon as the guy came out to look at erecting some stables for me as the horse is coming home. He is going to put the stables up at the end of September so Tremezzo will be able to come home then. It will be good exercise for me every day, as the stables will be approximately ¼ mile from the house up the fields. I will have to go up and down there at least five or six times a day to him, plus riding him out and doing all the stable work, so I shall be kept fit through the winter. I truly believe this is the secret of staying healthy, keeping toned and not having too large granny wings. Although I do have granny wings under my arms they are not as bad as they would be if I were not riding and doing the manual work around the stables.

1st August leave for Prague today, now at Heathrow and waiting for my girlfriend Sarah, whose daughter is in the Junior British Team. Great excitement as we haven't seen each other properly to catch up for a very long time. Both as daft as light still and nearly managed to get on the wrong plane. Drove from Prague to where the competition is being held, staying in a filthy dirty hotel along with all the other team members, but it is nice to be back at top level eventing and enjoying myself with horsey people. Sarah is neat and tidy, still dieting like mad and she said how fit I look, so feel really good about that. I am three years younger than Sarah and probably fitter than her ,but I wouldn't have been if I were carrying as much weight as I had been two years ago.

4th August cross country day and it is pouring with rain. Sarah's husband has hired a box at the race course and we have been in there all day watching the horses going round the cross country, very pleased he has done so because it is raining cats and dogs. I have on two coats, a pair of leggings underneath my jeans, two t-shirts and a sweater and I am still frozen, so is everybody else and it is August! I thought Prague was supposed to be a warmer country but it doesn't seem warm at the moment. Have eaten quite a large bar of chocolate today, Sarah and I had a bar each because Alice did so well. It was our form of celebration we decided we would prefer that to a bottle of champagne. Driving was a bit hairy with Sarah today so I have been driving and she read the map much better! When I am stressed I want to eat and Sarah's driving makes me feel very stressed!

6th August, my late father's birthday and flown back from Prague. We have come back with fleas, how can someone who is as meticulous as me with hygiene come back with fleas? But the whole British Team and all the supporters have. Steve made me strip off at the airport and put all my clothes in a white bag, he gave me a clean set of clothes to come home in. When we reached home and he took my clothes out of the white bag into a bucket there were fleas still in the bag so goodness knows what it is like for the people who got on the plane after us. We all knew we had got them, there wasn't a lot we could do about it. It was down to the hotel. My feet were bitten and my forehead from sleeping on my tummy. I tried to eat a little of the aeroplane food and something lodged making me very sick. I think flying has something to do with what I can and can't eat because the whole trip I have had a job to eat anything. Thank goodness I had some cuppa soups and Options hot chocolate with me otherwise I think I would have starved to death. Anyway I don't think I have lost any weight over it, but flying certainly does affect the band, I am sure of that.

Back in the office on the 7th August, how I hate the office and also starving hungry as I have not been able to keep much down at all over the past week. This morning I had some very watery porridge, two cups of cuppa soups and two Options hot chocolates. Now feel much better.

9th August everything is running true to form, the computer has packed up, been on to PC World, stress, stress, stress, cheese & onion crisps and a bar of chocolate straight down the hatch. What am I going to do with myself? However, tomorrow is another day.

13th August now taken part in 30 mile ride today, feel very fit, feel good, horse is fit and food isn't bothering me today thank goodness but I am sure on the way home I will have something from the garage, and yes, I have, I had a milk chocolate Mars drink and a packet of cheese & onion crisps. When I arrived home Steve had cooked me spaghetti bolognaise mince with wholemeal spaghetti (which is the only type of spaghetti I can eat) as the band does not like ordinary spaghetti. I had a very good day and life is good. Spoke to Thomas and he is not enjoying his job so much. I don't want to be stressed, it is late at night and I shall just go to sleep and think about getting into a size 10 that will stop me eating.

21st August woke up absolutely ravenous, quite a stressful day ahead of me Unit 4 is moving into Unit 3, stress really does it to me. I don't know why it does but it makes me want to eat all the time. Thank goodness I cannot stuff my face with masses and masses of cream cakes, potatoes & chips, fried fish and all the things I used to eat loads of sausages at the rate of knots, beefburgers and McDonalds because I would be down there today. So, on the positive side I haven't been able to do that, had porridge for breakfast, a ham sandwich at lunch time (part of it lodged, part of it didn't) and tonight I had tuna with a jacket potato, finely chopped beetroot and sweetcorn. Thoroughly enjoyed it and rounded it off with a cup of Options hot chocolate.

24th August my friend Ged has been in to see me today and he was amazed at how good I am looking. I am getting very boring by saying how good people are saying I am looking but it is true and I am proud of it thank you Mr Appleton, things are absolutely wonderful. Scrambled egg for breakfast this morning, a slice of toast with a cuppa soup for lunch and a packet of cheese & onion crisps mid afternoon – shouldn't have done that I do know but I cannot give them up. They are like a drug, it must be the salt, I am not sure what it is but I cannot give them up! Maybe I will try some hypnotherapy or something. I also had a can of cider this evening but I feel very good and the eating is under control overall. I am not eating huge amounts, unable to due to the band.

27th August been to Upton St. Leonard's, Barnsley Castle in Cirencester for a 30 mile ride and race, finished second so feel very pleased with myself. I was beaten by a 22 year old so what can you expect. This evening went to Barnsley House, Bibury near Cirencester (about 2 miles up the road from where the race ride was) very handy, to a concert in the grounds along with some friends and we had a great time. I have eaten very carefully, soup to start with, followed by white fish and a cappuccino. So now have the hang of eating out in public, it has taken me nearly two years. I stick to very safe things that I know will slide down. I never eat bread when I am out in company because if I do it lodges, not only because I don't chew it properly, but it doesn't like the band. If I am talking and eating I seem to have great trouble digesting the food. That side of things hasn't become any better and I don't know how to deal with it.

28th August Bank Holiday, out with Thomas and having a lovely time, been to Starbucks, that goes down nice and easily. He had a Panini, I didn't, how about that for will power but I knew very well it would make me sick and it stresses him if he sees me vomiting because of the band. Although he says it is money well spent and that is from another Doctor!

30th August, have been shopping today and bought a new kitchen for one of the flats in Aylesbury, very pleased with my purchase. I felt nimble when I went to ride the horses this afternoon as the mounting block had been dismantled so had to leap on from the fence. Thoroughly enjoyed it, it was great going up the gallops today. Feel good and the hip is not painful so that is even better.

2nd September have ridden all week and had a real horsey day today, feeling fit, feeling good and we ate out this evening with some friends. I had pate to start with (no toast) just on it's own with a slither of tomato, haddock on mustard mashed potato and a cappuccino. Note I have given up the Irish coffees, I also had two white wine spritzers, can't give those up, life wouldn't be worth living.

4th September great excitement the horses' shavings have arrived ready for his bed, also the hay is stacked in the field ready, feeling very excited about Tremezzo coming home. Will have to keep the weight off to ride him because he is only a little flat horse and his top weight he can carry is 11 stone, so I don't want to be getting back up there if I can help it.

6th September horror of horrors dentist today – stress – can't bear the dentist, eaten a packet of cheese & onion crisp, fatal. Mr Brocklehurst, who I have been going to for some 20 years or more, says my teeth surprisingly for the amount of sweets I eat are not too bad at all and no fillings this time – wonderful.

7th September, been riding but no Debbie in the office, so I had to go in the office today and have I got behind with the work. Have been nibbling all day, I made a couple of sandwiches and ate those. Taken all day to eat, one was ham, the other cheese. I grate the low fat cheese and try to watch the calorie intake from the cheese. I do not eat much blue cheese any longer and I have more or less stopped eating cheese whereas at one point I was eating huge amounts of it. And I mean slabs I don't mean your usual piece you buy at the supermarket I am talking about a great big chunk from Costco. How disgusting is that just eating neat fat!

9th September the school reunion. I met my friend Dawn and we had a great time.

10th September, met up with Vince, whose horses I am going to help look after through the winter and in return he is going to come and do some gardening for us. Marched across the fields, he could hardly keep up with me so we had a bit of a laugh about that especially as he is about 10 years younger than me, and then I realised I was supposed to be meeting somebody back at the farm so I ran back to the car and was amazed at how much energy I have. Feel fantastic.

11th September and Sean, the guy from the hunt has come to put a hunt gate in the field. He was mortified that he had to walk across four fields. I mean he is a country guy and he hasn't any energy at all. So we will watch this space to see what sort of mess he makes of putting the gate in. Starving hungry this evening and have eaten two cuppa soups and three Ryvita, plus sweetcorn, chopped up beetroot and tomato (little bit of vegetable please note).

12th September stress levels have dropped, Debbie is back and hopefully she will manage to get me straight again in the office as I have managed to create a mess. Also had a delivery from Pearce's today, with horse equipment so feel on very good form. The guy came to empty the cesspool. My does it smell – awful – that is the Klargester for the site and the house. Thought you would like to know that Mr Appleton. I also recommended to scented Sid the lorry drive that he visit you because he is about 7 stone overweight. He earns plenty of money and he could afford it.

14th September out to lunch with Jenny, the lady whose horses I ride as it is the end of the season. We had a lovely lunch I had prawns & chicken breast with garlic mayonnaise and for my main course chicken in white wine sauce with a little sliced tomato from a salad, very nice it was too. Only sparkling mineral water to drink and a cappuccino, still no Irish coffees. We went for a walk around Waddesdon Gardens, had a lovely walk, saw the beautiful birds. Did not go into the shop for a cup of tea and a piece of cake afterwards, very tempted to because the carrot cake looked absolutely delicious but as I had managed to survive the lunch without pukking I didn't want to go and risk having something and making Jenny wonder what was the matter.

CHAPTER 8

Healthy, Trim & Fit

20th September out to dinner with Peter and Helen, haven't actually eaten out with Helen before so extra careful, although Peter is a regular visitor to us. Very careful what I ate, I had king prawns to start, chewed them properly to ensure I did not choke or get them stuck, followed by a shepherd's pie it was OK so ate very carefully. Two white wine spritzers, normal standard procedure and no coffee tonight. Helen is a fit looking lady, so pleased I am also fit because I would have felt very uncomfortable sat with her in my old state as she is neat and trim. That is when it really feels beneficial to have gone through what I have so I never feel awkward or out of place any more.

21st September Thame show, had a good walk around there, didn't have any of the naughties like freebies they give away, test this chocolate, these crisps, didn't do it. Picking is the worst thing and I managed not to do it, it is bad enough having the weakness of cheese & onion crisps without picking at freebies at horse shows.

Sunday 24th September lovely week-end Thomas home, he looks absolutely dreadful, tired, exhausted, worn out. Says he is enjoying the job but has done nothing but sleep and eat since he got home, he is desperately thin and well, all I can say is he looks a mess. We have been to Starbucks together and out to lunch at The Angel where the food was mediocre. Ate very carefully, had leek & potato soup then haddock on mashed potato and a couple of Brussell sprouts (made a change) for lunch. It has been a lovely week-end although I was up early to go riding I have had a very restful day today.

25th September Monday, a very busy day today. Have been to the new flat, seen the electrician, carpenter and the plumber. Good job I am fit or I would never keep up the pace. If it was back in the old days I would be absolutely exhausted and dying to get into bed but as it happens I am now going riding. I am sure I shall have a great ride because been cooped up and horribly busy all day.

27th September Steve and I have flown to France today for a long week-end. It is boiling hot, we picked the little car up, drove to the bed & breakfast we are staying in. It took us two hours because we flew to Perpignan and needed to get to Carcassonne where we are hoping to buy a small apartment, very exciting, keep off the food because all the French women are shapely, their clothes are tiny and beautiful. Have been very sick tonight, must be the flying, haven't been able to keep a single thing down. I only had vegetable soup, it wasn't liquidized but it was well mashed, this made me sick, went to have a tiny piece of chicken and couldn't keep that down. I couldn't even keep a cup of hot chocolate down, not very good today.

28th September, fabulous apartment we have seen, hope we are going to be able to buy it, agent is damn rude but that hasn't spoilt the lovely lunch Steve and I had even though I haven't been able to keep any food down. We really enjoyed our day today, drove all around the village and going to make an offer. The area is fantastic and the apartment overlooks the Pyrenees, an hour and a half from the Pyrenees to go skiing and an hour and a half to go swimming in the sea how great is that?

30th September have been swimming in the sea today and yesterday we drove to the Pyrenees, just cannot believe how lovely this place is, feeling good but still unable to eat very well. So from that point of view it will be a good thing when we get home because I forgot to bring any soups although we have been and bought me some crisps but they are not the same as Walkers so they don't appeal to me quite the same. However, I am sure I will be alright, I won't starve to death, I haven't lost any more weight and life is good. We walked 6 miles today feel great as we have been doing a lot of driving around in the car and that makes me constipated. This makes me feel fatter and bloated. So, I am pleased we have had a good bit of exercise today. Makes me feel good in myself if I exercise.

1st October flown home today and still can't eat anything apart from had a cup-a- soup. Do feel a bit headachy and drunk lots of water to make sure I don't dehydrate. Don't really know what is going on at the moment, but I am sure I will be alright tomorrow.

4th October feel a lot better today than I have done for a few days. I managed to keep scrambled egg down this morning and I had two cuppa soups for lunch. Cabbage, gravy, mashed potato and half a chicken breast this evening, all kept down. Made me feel a lot better, I was starting to feel a little panicky, but it is the flying, I am sure it is the flying. I will have to put up with the discomfort as I am not going to give up travelling and

I am not going to have the band removed so I will be persevering.

5th October hair cut again today and Francine has lost another 3lbs since I last saw her she is doing well without the band. I am glad I haven't had to struggle like she has.

6th October I am feeling great today, I am eating properly, well as normal as I do anyway since I had the band fitted. I haven't been sick for the last 3 days and I feel like my old self, although I do look black under the eyes. I must make sure I drink plenty of water when I am having bouts of not being able to eat anything properly so I don't dehydrate. I am aware of what I need to do it's putting it all into practice.

9th October and Thomas is 26 today. I am heavier today than I was when I gave birth to him, which is ironic, however, that is life and what can you say – it is difficult. I am glad I am not still as big as I was 2 years ago because that would have been even more depressing, but at least I am fit and I wouldn't want to be as skinny as I was before I had Thomas. I was a bit too small and probably would look very old and withered. Am I kidding myself here! Thomas is working and it is the first birthday I haven't seen him so that is a little disappointing.

10th October I have been to see Thomas in London and have eaten out this evening. It was horrendous on the train, people smelling of B.O because it was so hot and some very large people, all I wanted to say to them was do some exercise, get a band fitted, do some exercise, get a band fitted. It sounds slightly prejudiced but it is the only way, exercise and cut the volume of food down. If you can't do it naturally then you have to have help. There was a programme on the television over the week-end, a sitcom, the guy was saying about how fat people smell and how fat people are thick and how fat people don't walk they waddle, it all sounded very cruel and very harsh but it is true and I know because I have been there. I never ever want to go back there, never. Now home and been up and down to see Tremezzo four or five times today it is fantastic to have him back to ride him when I feel like it. It will keep me very fit running up and down to the stables. The dogs Guinness & Gloucester will lose some weight so he is a good asset regarding fitness for the whole household.

14th October quite stressed today eaten a lot of junk, stress due to flat being purchased and having to be modernized, workmen are a nightmare. However, making progress, hopefully diet will be better tomorrow.

15th October out to lunch, had tomato soup to start, chicken for my main course, managed to eat broccoli and carrots, unfortunately none of it stayed down. Had a good ride out on Tremezzo in the afternoon, eaten Slim-a-soup, cheese & onion crisps and 3 Ryvita - all stayed down.

19th October another stressful day, eating habits not so bad apart from eating my porridge too quickly, it lodged, had to throw up, started again and kept it down. In total two whole tablespoons. Day taken up with the Planning Officer, carpet layers and Tremezzo. On the go all day and very tired.

20th October leave for Germany & Poland today. A rare trip for us by coach, both of us are apprehensive as prefer to travel on our own rather than with other people. Only booked it as it is one of the few tours that visits Colditz and where the Great Escape took place.

Off to a fine start, child sat behind me on feeder coach kicking my seat! Glad I am not still obese as would not fit down the aisle – very narrow – in fact I am able to walk forwards normally up the coach. Great feeling of achievement!
At the ferry, Dover – picked up silver service coach, doesn't look any different to the one we have just got off! But no kids – that's a blessing.

Had a great lunch in restaurant on ferry unable to believe how smart it is. Ate grilled tuna & broccoli soup, two glasses of Chardonnay. Missed coach – say no more. Eindhoven picked up coach again! Already blacklisted for rest of trip as held coach up for over an hour at Calais!

22nd October many pleasant people on trip, probably no long life buddies but some are good fun and at least they are now all speaking to me again. Once upon a time I would have turned to chocolate for comfort but not now, just a bag of cheese & onion crisps – only half the calories – only joking Mr Appleton but many a true word spoken in jest.

23rd October amazing to see Colditz although the outside has been renovated, it is still very easy to see how cramped the prisoners of war were here. No fat prisoners all looking starved in the pictures – poor devils. Very glad to have some exercise.

24th October Dresden – beautiful city, fabulous theatre land and restaurants, wonderfully clean. Great to be off the coach. There is one family from Leeds, woman called Michelle, all she can speak about is McDonalds and chip butties, has arse the size of a house, must weigh 18 to 19 stone. I feel like Twiggy thank goodness. I would like to tell her about the band but it is none of my business if she wants to eat herself to death, but I could not bring myself to sit near her for breakfast, just seeing her stuffing the food down, heaps of bacon, croissants, jam, sausages by the bushel – made me feel sick, but once I was like her and being honest sometimes would still like to eat the odd bacon sandwich but not six in a row!

25th October glad it is the last day on the coach. Thoroughly enjoyed seeing Stalleg Lft 3 prisoner of war camp where the Great Escape took place. Poland is still very poor and basic but the people friendly. Good to have some proper exercise, soon feel very bloated and constipated. Have eaten 2 ham rolls today and drunk 1 litre of water – not enough – must drink more as have pain in lower back, could be kidneys. Haven't wanted to drink as not keen to use coach loo!!! Arrived in Berlin at 6.30pm, had excellent meal with people we have met. Beautiful grilled Doyle fish, also a little spinach – note still off the Irish coffee, had a cup of cappuccino instead.

27th October - day in Berlin – have visited twice before so had a lazy time, just as well as not feeling too good, may be due to alcohol last night. Had a good walk round, haven't been able to keep anything down today. I had smoked salmon for breakfast – normally fine but not today. Tried some tuna & sweetcorn for lunch – no definitely not a good day for eating, able to feel it lodged, only one answer and that is to throw up. Dinner a little better, ate grilled fish but nothing else – feel very tired. Unable to blame flying for band tightening as this time didn't fly! Probably full that's why unable to eat as had very little exercise.

28th October light headed, lethargic, difficulty in concentrating. Have enjoyed holiday but glad to be going home, feel rather weak, probably down to poor diet over a period of twenty months. Eaten very little greens, must up my game. Need to replace crisps with something more nourishing. I know only too well it is the salt I crave. For someone who is so strong willed I have no idea why I am unable to correct my diet. Deep down probably do not want to.

Have felt mentally tired this trip, my mind has not been very active – unusual for me when having a break – slight pains in chest, need to see Alan Watt?

Great to visit Check Point Charlie again – last time I was here was in 1994 with my late husband Bill and son Thomas.

Have eaten very little this trip but also very little exercise. Enjoyed the sights but probably would not do this type of holiday again, Steve would. Glad to be flying home, can't wait to ride out and see the dogs this afternoon. Not looking forward to being back in the office on Monday. Now sat on BA flight next to a bloke in women's clothes – enough to drive me to drink! And it isn't Steve.

1st November winter is here – very cold – I am not enjoying the riding so much, feeling the cold something terrible, have seen Sandra and she says the same. Hot low calorie soup all round. Do seem to be able to eat better.

5th November will have to buy myself some winter clothes, everything looks like a sack on me – nice feeling. Rode on the gallops today, very cold – soon warmed up by second lot. Looking forward to meeting the other people, at the Shelburne on Tuesday evening as I have never spoken to anyone else who has had the operation besides Sandra.

6th November my appetite seems to be enormous today, have eaten two rounds of Marmite sandwiches, 2 tablespoons porridge oats, 1 cup-a-soup, 2 hot chocolates, 2 tablespoons sweetcorn, 3oz ham, 1 small jacket potato, ½ pint smoothie – really into the 100% fruit smoothies. Still off the junk, no crisps and no chocolate – fantastic – long may it last.

28th November went to the gallops today, rode Pendle Hill an Aintree prospect, he is all horse, 16 hands 3in huge chaser, I'm like a pea on a drum. He and I went up those gallops at Lambourne like the wind. I didn't think I would ever pull him up, good work out on the stomach, toning of arms and legs etc! Even my bum feels much tighter, don't think I will hardly be able to walk tomorrow! He was the most powerful horse I have ridden in the last 2 years, could not have managed him a year ago.

29th November feel good, not even stiff, must be fitter than I thought. Will go to party on Friday feeling well toned! Hair has more or less stopped falling out, feel very good.

1st December Alice's 21st party, wonderful to have worn a handkerchief dress looking fit and healthy and not like a frumpy beached whale. There were so many slim young beauties there it was fantastic not to feel old and huge.

Two years ago I did not believe it would ever be possible. We danced all night and had a great time - feeling a million dollars.

3rd December my son Thomas took me out for lunch for my birthday tomorrow. Had cauliflower & broccoli soup, haddock & mash, 1 white wine spritzer, no coffee as felt too full, I didn't want to be sick.   Long gone the Irish coffees!

4th December Yuk 54 years old today – grim – but they say you are only as old as you feel, well I am pleased to say I feel as if I have been re-born. Had a great ride on Tremezzo, worked all day in the office then Steve took me out to dinner. Still pretty full from yesterday's lunch so ate minimal.

5th December looking forward to BOSPA meeting tonight. It's good to hear what others have to say re: all their hopes and fears. No-one was more hopeful & fearful than myself. Strange how I can relate to every word others say.

Having arrived, I thought there would be more there although a good turn out. A booklet was handed round that will be promotional material pre-op. I hated the figure on the front, mainly because it was faceless. Yes I was one of those that felt faceless whilst the size of a beach whale, but of course I was not, that was only one of many negative thoughts. The picture needed a face in my opinion, the rest was ok but on the last page a smiling face again would have helped. I realise the picture is portraying how fat people feel, faceless, lonely, isolated, not taken seriously, but for me the brochure does need to motivate by the last page.

I was surprised to hear a couple of people say that from the moment they were pushed into the theatre Mr Appleton's words had a great impact on them regarding their way of thinking about food. Have to confess although I knew it was the day to change my life for ever I didn't believe it, very relieved to have been proved wrong. Going under for me - I was already trying to cheat the band, if I melt the Mars Bars, if I liquidize steak & kidney pies, if I chop up pasta to pin head size ..... However, nearly 2 years later, I never liquidize anything. I now have 100 grams of detox smoothie Innocent Brand made of 100% berries and fruit for breakfast, a sandwich for lunch – low fat hard cheese with a tomato (takes me ¾ hour to eat otherwise it lodges), fish & veg for dinner. Still eat 2 packets of cheese & onion crisps a week and 2 Crunchies (much better than Mars Bars as only 196 calories instead of 500). It would be better not to eat any I know but it is better than eating 6 packets of crisps and 3 Mars Bars a day. This has taken time I realise now, but I had not realised this until tonight after listening to others. The person next to me, Nicki, had the band fitted 18 months ago, she said she'd just had another fill to 8½ml. Having looked back in the diary I also went back to Mr Appleton to have a top up to 8½ml but he talked me out of it. As he was able to do this deep down I could not have really wanted it tightened. Being very strong willed if I had definitely wanted the extra ½ml I would have pushed for it until I had my own way. I am very relieved I listened to him as I am able to eat a little when I go out and although I still have days where I vomit because I haven't chewed properly, or because I haven't eaten all day and eaten too quickly, food no longer dominates my thoughts.

It was interesting to hear a lady say how she plans her holiday around the restaurants, I used to do that, how bad is that? Now I am relieved to say I focus on what activities there are and sights to see.

Positive Outcome

Exercise has been such a major player for me since the operation. The love of horses, hiking and skiing has been my inspiration. I so often think of the Christmas before I had the operation when I sat at the top of a mountain in Obergurgl like a mountain on a mountain while downing plates of pasta, mugs upon mugs of hot chocolate with brandies, while my family skied outside on the mountain. Very different a year later, first out every morning, last in of a night, feeling fit and free. Pleased to report feeling the same way now but even fitter! Great.

6th December Glad I have kept this diary as I am becoming complacent of what I have achieved, my mind set is this is normal and I am very relieved I have it in writing. All the negativity that drove me to the operation I would never ever want to forget. I didn't think I would ever be able to say that but I can with confidence. It all seems a life time ago but it is only 2 years.

Tremezzo was fresh today had a good work out while riding him so can continue not riding the bike thank goodness.

15th December can't wait for Xmas break, eating too much chocolate again need to stop – unable to!

16th December had lunch with Steve's mum & Cedric. Now in control of the eating out – answer CHOOSE CAREFULLY.

17th December had lunch with Brenda & Graham (my sister & her husband) who know nothing of band – had to have soup to start in case anything lodged followed by fish cake. Both stayed down. The amount I am eating must be approximately a tenth of what it used to be.

20th December had lunch with Debs & Sandra. I chose very carefully so as not to throw up. Had soup, pheasant (no veg) and custard for pud. All stayed down.

Had a call from a neighbour who has never been out of the village, well except to Thame cattle market. When I asked how he was he said 'not too bad but he has been having an affair' (the mind boggles - although a lovely bloke he still wears jumpers that his mum knitted for him with sheep on the front). After this piece of news I asked him why he was letting me know and he said well I was a woman (as if he has only just noticed after 30 years) and he wanted to know if he should tell his partner of 15 years who also comes from the village. When I enquired how long the affair had been going on for he said about 18 months. I replied that if this was the case his partner would know – woman's intuition and all that. His reply was 'well if she already knows then he had no need to tell her!' For once I did not have an answer, so had a white wine spritzer instead.

24th December attended church for carol service, freezing cold, followed by pub – nice & warm!

26th December rode on gallops two lots, horses fresh, thoroughly enjoyed the exercise after all the food yesterday. Mood swings have definitely stopped not had one for over a year.

30th December Steve's birthday, went for an Indian meal, managed to eat then threw up. Chicken korma and rice did not sit well. Thomas said with authority I didn't chew it properly! Unfortunately he was right. I thought I had learned – obviously not – needed a reminder.

31st December great New Year's Eve, first one in the UK for 9 years, was dreading it but pleasantly surprised. Went to our pal's restaurant - Angelo's and all were in great form, drank too much champagne – Taxi home.

1st January 2007 New Year not having to go on the obligatory diet is fantastic. To be honest with myself, would like to lose another stone but in reality will settle for 7lbs. This last 7lbs does seem hard to achieve but as I still eat sweets it is hardly surprising. All I would have to do is cut them out but I love them and I feel good so not going to worry too much.

2nd January have I over eaten over Xmas…..No only 2 mince pies and that was to be polite to my elderly neighbours. Used to love mince pies but they made me feel sick much to my relief. Xmas day had a little duck with apple sauce and one slice of turkey with gravy, no pud. The Xmas day lunch did nothing for me whatsoever.

3rd January went to the BOSPA meeting last night, learned a lady has 8½ml still and is coping. Don't know whether I would or not. Few people there, one new person unable to make her mind up whether to have the operation or not.

Egypt – Bikini Holiday

4th January, off to Sharm-El-Sheikh in Egypt. Early start, 4.00am, had a hot chocolate to drink in case the band tightens in mid air and unable to eat. Arrived at the 5* All Inclusive (I think not) straight for the dining room as both of us starving. First thing that struck me almost everyone was very over weight. As Steve pointed out people book all inclusive so they can eat all day long with no extra cost! Starving I may be but food not great – had chicken soup and rice with gravy/wine sauce. All stayed down so band not tightened only a little as able to eat about 2 tablespoons of rice before feeling full.

5th January rude awakening 'Morning Campers' in 5 different languages booming over the tannoy at 10.00am opposite our room. Hangover at it's best.

This budget break may be not such a good idea as tannoy finished only to be followed by planes taking off every 30 minutes, followed by a break of about 3 hours to be followed by planes taking off every 30 minutes! It gets worse the gym was absolutely awful so no proper exercise for a week. Personally I confess I am relieved as the sun is hot, pool is quiet as away from the tannoy and a very slim, fit, little waiter waiting on me hand and foot with drinks as I lay on my sun bed in the much dreamed about bikini.

6th January hot, no aches and pains and a massage – great day doing nothing except reading and sunbathing – also drinking. It is great to get away and not have my thoughts dominated by food.

7th January – general pattern of food intake –

9.00am – hot chocolate (Options – took them with me)
10.00am – pitta bread, toasted cheese
11.30am – mineral water
12.30pm – rice and some form of sauce – 2 tablespoons
2.00pm – mineral water
3.00pm – a little grilled fish – 2 tablespoons
4.30pm – hot chocolate (Options)
6.00pm – gin & tonic
7.30pm – chicken, rice & sometimes soup
8.30pm – midnight – 3 white wine spritzers

No deserts as did not fancy them. Once I would have been eating everything in sight as well as buying more. Instead of being first through the restaurant doors we would amble in after a drink at the bar.

11th January to summarize our week - the most exercise I have had was getting on and off the sunbed. Steve, who is not fond of the sun managed to have a stomach bug, catch a cold, walk into a glass door on the patio, fall off the side of the road and graze his shoulder & arm plus buy a new made to measure suit for the cost of £85.00 (the only thing that went right for him the whole trip except he ordered 2 and only one came)!

13th January full of cold and very chesty, now on antibiotics and feel terrible no energy. Just learnt Sarah has booked us a ski trip for a week to Gargellen, Austria for early February. Hope I feel fitter than I do now otherwise I will not be going.

18th January - on the mend - have been on treadmill for 40mins at 6.2, burned 350 calories. Nearly killed me, so unfit after three weeks without any exercise, legs feel like jelly.   Had a chicken breast with carrots & peas for dinner.

20th January, been on treadmill each day.   Eating a lot, 6 slices of bread throughout the day, 1 tin baked beans, ¼ cucumber, 6 tspns Bertolli spread, 2oz grated low fat cheese, 4 mugs low calorie Options hot chocolate, 1½ litres of water, 1 Crunchie, NO CRISPS.

21st January rode out three horses today, 40 minutes on treadmill, ate much the same as yesterday, feel knackered – early night.

22nd January worked in office all day. Do feel much better for exercising but diet not brilliant, more or less same as 20th January but ate home made vegetable soup for lunch. Made appointment to meet Mr Appleton on the 20th February 2007 with view to having band tightened.

27th January up bright and early, excited as going to Point to Point. Can't wait to see Pendle Hill run, I have enjoyed working him on the gallops.

Long day, very cold, Pendle ran very well; think he will win next time.   Tried to eat a venison burger but unable to digest it.

1st February new figure, no mood swings for ages and hair cut short today – first time in 13 years. Hope it will make me weigh less!

3rd February, Rush, Rush, Rush. Rode out 3, put Peps out in field, Sandra came, feel exhausted. Glad to be going away tomorrow. Made appointment to have band tightened. Nervous about it but must be done! I can eat far too many sandwiches one and a half rounds no problem. Taking Chromium herbal tablets – not wanting chocolate – let's hope it lasts.

4th February met Sarah at Stanstead for a girlie ski week in Gargellen, Austria. We had both been 36 years ago in our teens, both looking forward to it. Neither of us like cattle truck airways! Hotel Madrisa as we remembered it, food excellent know I am going to put on weight, fab food, fab skiing, sunny and warm.

5th February good breakfast, cottage cheese, ham & hot chocolate. Skied until 1.00pm, good conditions, great fun, not crowded by any means but resort much larger. Goulash soup for lunch, band did not like this! Good job too as full of calories. Gluvine x 2, great skiing in the afternoon. Met some other English – great fun.

7th February skied all day, fantastic, feel so fit and well. The alcohol is making me put on weight, am having a little trouble keeping food down and have done so the last couple of days. Had lunch with some Swiss people – excellent fun. So good to be in such a lovely place with lovely people.

8th February text from Thomas he has passed his exam for surgery, very pleased with himself and so am I – very pleased with him! Went to an opera night up the mountain, sat with 5 other English guys from Yorkshire. They were better than any comedy show – average age 64 years! Like Sarah pointed out only seven years older than her and only 10 years older than me. Many drinks, many laughs and a lot of good food. Unfortunately it all stayed down. Definitely need the band tightening.

9th February last night, met up with everyone for a drink after dinner. The waitress won't be getting a tip from us, she is like Miss Kleff in the James Bond film. Keep expecting to see a flick knife come out of the toe of her shoe – my word she is evil. Not one day has passed where she hasn't given us an order "you will be at dinner for 7.30pm, you will have 5 courses like it or not!" Long time since someone has tried to tell me what to do, fortunately she gave Sarah and I the giggles. Would I go back? Yes, beautiful place.

10th February back to reality flying home at tea-time but no skiing this morning as did not want to tempt fate. My hand has only just mended and my chest is now clear so it will be nice to return home in one piece and feeling 100% fit but rather fat. Probably put on 6lbs. Time will tell will weigh on Monday.

12th February at my desk bored stiff, eating rice throughout the day, looking forward to having band tightened as lots of nice events to attend from end of March. Only put on 3lbs so now working to get it off.

18th February rode 4 horses on the gallops, feel exhausted. Very hungry afterwards, ate 1½ low fat cheese sandwiches but still off the chocolate and not tempted – how great is that! Lost 2lbs so Boots scales say – 1lb left on. One Chromium a day keeps the chocolate away!

20th February I have been to Mr Appleton at the Paddocks this evening to have the band tightened, another 1/2ml put in so I now have a total of 81/2mls. He was very pleased with me, I hadn't put on any weight in fact I had lost a further 2lbs. I can drink a glass of water with the band tightened and feel fine. I was very nervous as hoped

I would never have to have a fill again. As he rightly says it will not stop me feeling bored whilst sat at my desk and picking at chocolate or anything else liquid high calorie, all it will do is stop me eating large amounts. I have to keep reminding myself of this.

21st February feel bright as a button this morning the band has restricted my eating capacity, could only eat half a slice of pitta bread this morning with a little spread. Feel good, very relieved I have had it tightened and know it was the right move.

23rd February had two girlfriends come to lunch today, Wendy & Pauline, quite nerve racking worrying whether I am going to be able to eat in front of them. I cooked a shepherd's pie and managed to push enough around my plate. Not able to swallow much but had a very long lazy lunch, walked out to see the horse, really enjoyed ourselves, the chatter was good and nobody noticed that I couldn't eat hardly any food so that was great.

24th February week-end and been riding five horses this morning, three of them up the gallops, feel full of energy and looking good even if I say it myself, really enjoying being agile at the age of 54.

28th February Steve and I left to go to Eaux Bonnes in France today. We left home at five o'clock this morning, landed and the vehicle we were given was not up to standard as they have had so much snow here, we had to turn around to collect another vehicle, a four wheel drive, so hopefully the skiing will be good tomorrow with all the snow. Hardly able to eat any of the lovely food in the hotel tonight but I would rather be unable to eat than be fat. It is a small price to pay.

1st March and what a way to spend the first of the month out on the slopes, beautiful powder snow, we were on the slopes by ten o'clock and didn't pack up until four o'clock as the lifts shut down, what a wonderful day we both had. We skied for England, had a lovely lunch up the mountain, I had home-made broccoli soup and Steve had steak & chips. This evening had more home-made soup, I was really hungry so glad they had a nice wholesome soup for me to eat tonight.

4th March flew home after several good days, we have now bought a property in Eaux Bonnes, a beautiful little two bedroom apartment, hopefully it will all go through OK, time will tell, and let's hope it is not going to be stressful.

5th March have been to the BOSPA meeting, quite a good meeting Mr Farouk was there answering questions much the same as when we had the meeting with Sean Appleton, the same questions appear to keep coming up. I find the meetings a little repetitive but I think most people enjoyed the session this evening. I did enjoy it but it would also be good to have something new brought into the meetings.

8th March London today regarding letting one of the flats, quite stressful, very busy day, hardly eaten, had a cup of hot chocolate on the station going and a cup of hot chocolate on the way home, too tired to eat tonight, not good.

12th March changing banks after 35 years to another corporate bank in Oxford, very stressful, this has been going on for months now and goodness knows how many legal documents they want from me but my word it really is stressful and it makes me want to eat, thank goodness I have the band and I am unable to. I am so pleased I had the extra 1/2ml put in because I can only manage half a sandwich instead of eating two rounds, such a relief.

14th March been to Lambourne all morning, rode four racehorses up the mile, 4 furlongs, fantastic, how lucky I am to be alive, it was brilliant except when we returned to the lorry it was blowing a hurricane, really dangerous. I was relieved to put the horses on the lorry and climb into the cab myself. The horses went well and I don't even feel the slightest bit tired, fantastic.

Sunday 18th March I have ridden all week, feel fit, healthy and well. Steve and Thomas have been to the rugby and I went out with Sandra and had a Dover Sole, ate a quarter of it, what a waste of money, and one white wine spritzer.

21st March off to France today, bit disappointing we haven't managed to sign on the dotted line for the apartment today but hopefully it will all sort itself out, plenty of snow skiing wonderful, such lovely people in the Pyrenees. Long to spend more time here and to ski more often.

25th March home today had a fantastic time skiing, disappointed about the apartment not being signed for but hopefully it will happen at the end of April all being well, skied like a trouper for the four days.

28th March been to London today and met Judith, ate at a restaurant called the Lounge just off Regent Street, very nice, shame I couldn't eat the food. Couldn't find the toilet either because the door was hidden in wooden panelling and I needed to vomit, started to panic then fortunately somebody came out of the toilet door so I could see my way in. Thought I was going to have an accident but managed to survive. I had a good day, met Thomas & Steve afterwards so that was enjoyable, came back on the train, didn't get home until really late so it has been a long, long day. Looking forward to riding out tomorrow.

30th March another stressful day with the bank. I will be glad when this is over don't know why I am finding it so stressful as there is nothing really to be stressed about, apart from the amount of time it is taking and the amount of forms I have to fill in.

1st April fantastic day with the horses really enjoying them, wonderful to feel so fit and healthy. I have to say I am pleased with my short hair underneath my riding hat because it doesn't look half so messy when I take the hat off, just have to run my fingers through it. Sarah says I look a little elf like but that can't be helped.

Ate out tonight with some friends, and the planning officer who is dealing with my application for my new stable block. All looks good, had a lovely evening with them, chose my usual chicken but couldn't eat very much, in fact couldn't eat a quarter of it. Had one white wine spritzer and a cappuccino.

Monday 9th April it has been Easter week-end, I have had a fantastic time, went to the gallops every day. Have eaten 4 Easter eggs over the past few days. Now back on the straight & narrow.

11ᵗʰ April and I spoke to Sue regarding the motivational speaking at the next BOSPA meeting or at a BOSPA meeting, she is up for it so I will speak to Jo and see what she has to say. Hopefully she will be keen and I think it might help with the group sessions a little.

12ᵗʰ April two years three months have now passed since my operation. Life has changed dramatically for the better – beyond my wildest dreams. Not only do I feel trim, fit and healthy my mind is also far more active. I look forward to going out and meeting people love the sports I had so craved for - riding, skiing & hiking. The only thing I regret is I did not have the gastric band fitted much sooner! Thank you Mr Appleton for changing my life.